The Beginning
Rocky's Story: The Early Years

By Jack Hayword

Contents

Prologue

Let me introduce him; his name is Rocky and the following pages hold within them his life story as told by him; so let's hear what he has to say?

Rocky:

I have lived my life shadowed by several assumed identities. However, only one of them had catapulted me into wealth beyond any that I could have imagined on my own, and I have no clue to why me. What is clear I was borne to this earth no different from any other newborn unless one considers it was my fate is mistaken by my peers as being someone else other than myself? This phenomenon of assumed identity is lasting my entire life span. I have been mistaken for actors like Kirk Russell, Robert Taylor, and Robert Wagner; the singers have been Johnny Cash, and Elvis Presley. On television it is host Jay Leno. However, the person I have been mistaken for the most is actor Sylvester Stallone.

I am only divulging my story because it's an exciting story, different from billions of other reads worldwide. My story is rare; have you ever read of a person's lifestyle becoming a clone of genuine celebrities? I know of no other person who has gone from rags to riches as I have just because of my looks and relation to some Celebrity. I believe the reader will find the storyline to be a beautiful, healthy, compassionate, moving story. One hopes aboard the same Roller Coaster that I have been riding for a lifetime filled with criticism from my peers. Come and learn what many how crazed and foolish people reacted when they had convinced themselves I was the actual Celebrity they had perceived. or at least convinced themselves me out to be. I hope you will find here a story of passion, love, greed, sexual encounters, drugs, soul-searching, plus sadness, as well as a tale of tribulation over losses, besides newfound feelings that lead to triumph over diversity.

A personal note from the Author

We Humans are born and grow up with having unique personality; however, what if something or someone comes along and changes that? That something or someone for Rocky in his teen years was Elvis Presley. In his late twenties, it was Sylvester Stallone.

Since then, one consistent theme has remained. Whereby, through no choice of his, he would live a life of ambiguity, anger, redemptive hope, and seemingly genuine affection, yet sometimes terrifying by what he had been forced to endure. If his dysfunctional family did not drive him nuts, there were his peers who repeatedly identified him or assumed him for several Motion Picture Celebrities; Country Music singers, Comedians, Television Celebrities,' and many others.

As far as Rocky has always been concerned, he is just another person, not much different from most. His accolades from life so far have come mainly through his travels around the country. As for genuine love, it has continued to elude him because of the woman who comes into his life. Only there based on his celebrity and rumor related to one Celebrity.

No one controls him. Anyone knowing him knows you do not want to be the brunt of his evil side with him having a Black Belt in the Martial Arts. For his awareness of his peers, he knows the only reason they want to befriend him is for the same reason women only want him.

His peers, those who, upon meeting him, whomever they perceived him to be, through their egos block out any reasoning that the man is standing right in front of them could not be any other than their chosen Celebrity. Because of his peer's belief that their eyes would not deceive them, they are sure he had to be that very Celebrity. Unfortunately for him, because he is not that Celebrity, many of those who befriend him came to a rude awakening.

Rocky has always been of a chameleon with his looks; he seems to change them at his beckoning call. In his late twenties, more repercussions came to his life experiences. Where any personal life already afforded him was over, because of a Motion Picture titled after his sir name, 'Rocky.'

When he thought it is safe to come out of the water, someone yells, Shark. His lifestyle exploded, with Sharks all around him, and it all started the day he saw himself on a poster at the Lowes Theater in Nashville, Tennessee. So let's now join in an adventure that assures a front-row seat into Rocky's travels that gets him involved with all kinds of abuse. Along with the twist and turns of daily life, his many loves, hurts, and sacrifices he had endured. However, first we must at least read who Rocky is and how it was he became to be mistaken for those celebrations that influence his life. It is my hope you will enjoy his the Beginning.

Disclaimer
To whom it may concern:

The storyline that follows this disclaimer is an autobiographical story that mentions several celebrities. However, one get's mentioned more than others are, and that celebrity is Sylvester Stallone.

Any Celebrity who appears in the storyline was because of that Celebrity being some catalyst to some event. Otherwise, the storyline here is about me in its entirety, my life, times, and events, and my peers mistake me to be one of those celebrities.

One Celebrity prefers his name and image not to be used by anyone. And not used for others' monetary gain for any purpose, and that is Sylvester Stallone. However, that is not the case here. The storyline, being what it is, is not about him. However, because of Mr. Stallone's celebrity hood and likeness to me, is how I had gotten tucked into Mr. Stallone's shadow in the first place, and that affected my entire lifestyle and livelihood, not his.

Mr. Stallone, the actor, remains only in the story as a reference. However, any Celebrity I have mentioned throughout my story had nothing to do with the writing of the storyline. Therefore, they too are only a reference, and I made none of them pre-aware of the book's content.

Chapter 1: A Beginning

Glad you came along. Call me Rocky. I am from the State of Illinois, in the town of Sterling. A hamlet is resting alongside the 300 miles long Rock River; a non-navigable stream is rising in Washington County in Eastern Wisconsin and flowing in a southwesterly direction to join the Mississippi River at Rock Island. Along its banks stand other significant towns like Rock Falls, Watertown, Janesville, Beloit, Rockford, and Dixon. Upon a river bluff near Oregon stands Laredo Taft's 'Black Hawk,' a 48-foot statue of the Indian leader.

The day I arrived on the scene only if I would have been given a clue to how my life would be until my death, I would have known I was in for one hell of a ride. First, there was that feeling from that slap on my butt that brought with it screams and tears, all being inflicted upon me by someone holding me in the air by my feet.

If that was not wakening enough, the womb I had just gotten pulled from belonged to one of the wilder of two women I would soon come to know very well; the other being her sister, both born in a county of God-fearing farmers and God-fearing parents who are my Grandmother and Grandfather.

About the time when the Nineteenth Century headed into the Twentieth that Grandfather Dennis left Thurso Scotland heading for America. However, leaving one's homeland was one thing; what he did not consider is one does not walk onto a steam ferry at Ellis Island and departs in Brooklyn, New York, without having other relatives living there. However, realizing a first-time immigrant with limited funds in his pocket in a Scotch/Irish neighborhood is tight in the best of times. Leaving Scotland, he is a metallurgist and now finds himself to be just another immigrant. His type of work was about impossible to gain.

Maybe it is, let us say, the luck of the Scots that, through another immigrant, he learns of a factory in the town of Richmond, Kentucky. The problem was, it is a long way off, and therefore, he needed to get there to which he did by traveling by a team of road merchants, and they employed him to be in charge of the wagon's horses.

Shortly after he arrived in Richmond, he secured employment at the factory there. As months passed, life in the Americas is turning enjoyable and much more so when he befriends a man named John Milford Powell, another metallurgist.

My Grandmother, Nora Powell, is living south of Richmond in the hamlet known as Berea. Her father John invites Dennis to his home for the Sunday meal and on that day, he meets her; it is love in bloom. He and she saw something in one another, considering they took to courting another four years before getting married.

Nora was born in 1890 in Jackson County, Kentucky, to farmers John Milford Powell and Elizabeth Jane Coyle. Years after, Nora, John, and Elizabeth sold their farm and moved to Madison County, Kentucky. Within a few more years, they sold that farm and purchased another one in Berea.

Dennis and Nora brought forth five children, Bill, Park, Howard, Sylvia, and Ira. However, it is right after the birth of Ira when Dennis leaves his family. Without the slightest hint or even the courtesy of explaining his reasoning, one day, he is sitting at home in his favorite chair, and the next day, he is gone. Of course, this leaves the household without income, causing many hardships for Nora while feeding five children. Park and Ira were sent to live with their Grandparents, the Powell's.

Troublesome times or not, Nora was not another woman off some farm. She was culinary educated and extraordinarily creative person, and her first income getter is taking in the laundry. She started baking pies and doing the cooking for some of the town's elderly. The selling of her cakes that brought more money to the household than Dennis had ever provided.

Eight years would pass before Nora hears from Dennis in the way of him opening the screen door to the house one day, walked in, and headed straight for his favorite chair as if he had never left. Of course, Nora is on hand to question him about his whereabouts all those years;

however, he cowards up and had little to say. He just remained seated with a crap eating grin on his face.

What was for sure; Nora would never get an explanation behind Dennis's disappearing act, nor is there any explanation why Nora let him return. However, from that day forward, what's known there would not come a day for the rest of Dennis's life where Nora did not remind him of her eight years of hardships.

In days to come, it came apparent that he had gone to the town of Clinton, Iowa, during his departure, where he had been working in a factory and still maintained his employment there. Within days of returning home, he has packed up the family and moved them to Clinton. They would live there through the birth of another daughter, whom they named Marylou.

One day, a coworker tells Dennis that Northwestern Steel and Wire in Sterling, Illinois, are hiring, and the family is packing once again. In Sterling, where the family became the happiest and where their children had grown to be six. Out of the six, the wild ones were Park and Sylvia.

While working at Northwestern Steel and Wire, Dennis would befriend Joe, whose Christian name is Joseph? He had been a drifter of sorts, who had also heard that Northwestern Steel and Wire was hiring. He had previously worked in a factory in Saint Louis, Missouri, and had grown up over on a farm in Coulterville, Illinois, in the State's southern region.

There seemed to be some controversy concerning Joe's birth, to which his biological father might be. His parents were Italian immigrants; his Mother, Anna Mayo, is from Rome, and his father, Joseph, is from Palermo. They had settled in Coulterville, Illinois, where they had secured employment on a Bill and Greta Williams farm. Anna Mayo is their cook and housekeeper, while Joseph did the duties of a field hand.

Tragedy struck early one morning while Joseph plowed the north 60, and something spooked his plow horse. The horse rose on its hind legs, and when its front legs came down, they came straight down on Joseph and he got trampled to death. Of course, this leaves Anna Mayo, a widow.

With Joseph now buried, Bill and Anna Mayo had become lovers, of course, behind Greta's back. However, that is short-lived when tragedy struck again on a Sunday morning when Bill hitched up the buggy too, "Old Roily," the same plow horse that had killed Joseph and went the miles into the town of Marion. He spent the day playing cards over several glasses of white lightning with the boys at a local feed store. As some card games will do, someone cheated, and when this happens in Bill's game, he takes charge, and out of the ruckus, he is shot dead. When the news about Bill reached Coulterville, Greta is not the only one grief-stricken. However, Anna Mayo had not only lost her lover, but she is now pregnant.

When Greta learns of the pregnancy, she drives conclusions and assumes the Father was Bill; she never considered it might be Joseph's, thinking he had only passed a month before. Greta remained convinced it was Bill's and has dismissed Anna Mayo.

When Bill's death reaches his accomplished friend Villo Carmello, he also learns Anna Mayo's job had been ended. Mrs. Carmello had been in failing health for several years. That alone had destroyed any sexual relationship between her and Villo. With hearing the plight of Anna Mayo, he comes to her rescue and hires her as his housekeeper and Nanny to the Carmello children. However, as it was with Bill, Anna Mayo and Villo are also sleeping together and had been doing so for two months before Joseph's death; who knew?

Around the community, the rumor is that Anna Mayo might not be carrying Joseph's child; instead, it might be Bill's child, according to Greta's gossip. Then there were

Mrs. Carmello's thoughts of the child; it might be the doing of Villo's.

Despite those rumors, Anna Mayo continued to live and work for the Carmello's through the birth of a boy named after the late Joseph. However, the mystery remains; who is the birth Father, Joseph, Bill or Villo's? Who is Joe's biological father is one of those happenings in his life that would forever remain a mystery? During his years as a youth in Coulterville, his peers considered him a bastard child no matter what last name his mother had named him.

Upon Mrs. Carmello's death, when Joe is twelve, Anna Mayo became the new Mrs. Carmello. As the newlyweds were getting on with their lives, trouble is in the land, calling itself the "Great Depression." It hit unkindly on the Villo family, and it is not long before Villo's fortune was depleted. As the depression lingered, it brought hardship after hardship, and then Villo commits suicide. Young Joe had entered the barn that morning. He thought as he's approaching the door to the barn was how quiet it was. Usually, Villo would beat and banging while shaping horseshoes and the smell of the hearth wasn't in the air. Upon opening the barn door, the light of the sun came rushing in, directing its light on into the dark barn and right up to where Joe could see Villo hanging from a rafter. He stood there in a bit of shock because he had seen no one hanging before. He observed the rope is tight against the neck, and Villo's tongue is out of his mouth and clinging to one side, and his eyeballs looked as if they were about to pop out of their sockets. Gathering his senses, he runs to the house to tell Anna Mayo what he had just observed. For Anna Mayo, the death of Villo puts the burden of keeping the farm running and the raising of Joe and the two Carmello children.

In a few days, Joe would become seventeen, giving Anna Mayo cause to go to town to find a birthday present. However, she would have to walk to get there, considering their farm horse had dropped dead of old age just weeks before. Usually, Joe would hook up the buggy to the horse, and she would go to town. Without a horse, Anna Mayo had no other choice other than staying home and not getting Joe anything for his birthday and walked the three miles to reach the general store.

She finished her shopping and left the store to stop out on the store's wooden porch, admiring such a beautiful, warm day for November. Knowing she had the long walk home and getting there before nightfall, she crossed the dirt road that passed by the store and walked up to where the railroad crossing was. She looked up and down the tracks, and with not seeing any train approaching, she crossed. She was at the halfway point in the crossing when an oncoming train hits her. It was assumed she did not hear the whistle, and according to an eyewitness, the engineer gave its warning. Instead of getting out of the way, Anna Mayo turned directly into its path. Despite the screeching wheels and the whistleblowing, the front Cowcatcher hits her. Joe spends his birthday at the gruesome task with a basket in his hand, picking up his mother's remains; in fact, her head never was located; he and some bystanders thought maybe it had gotten smashed to pieces on impact.

With the death of Anna Mayo, the Carmello children concluded they had no need of Joe hanging around and suggested he move on. Of course, their decision was one he had expected, and therefore he had already packed by the time he heard the news. Joe never did like his step-siblings and was more than happy to depart the farm with his hopes filled with thoughts of a better life somewhere else down the road.

For the next few years, he traveled around the country like many of the unemployed were doing, hoping for one freight train after another. Eventually, one of them took him into Saint Louis; another one took him into Sterling.

When Dennis felt he had known Joe long enough to seal their friendship, he invited him to his home for the traditional after Church Sunday social meal. Of course, by accepting the invitation, Joe is sure to meet the rest of the family, which included wild Sylvia.

Of course, for Joe, its love at first sight; he barely had eaten when he's asking her for a date the following Saturday. Every Saturday hence was spent hanging out down by the Rock River, basking in the sun or wading in the cold water from their first date forward they became inseparable.

Most of her childhood remains a mystery, and maybe it should like the rumor she was having a sexual affair with her Brother Park of a continuing pattern that lasted right into adulthood. She would turn fifteen before her imagined sex life beyond Brother Park comes alive of its own accord, and without a plan, she struck out looking for her perfect man. His name was Dubb's? Who knew what attracted her; it might have been his deep blue eyes, broad shoulders, or maybe him being six-two with thick matted black hair. However, the one thing for sure that attracted the attention of this fifteen-year-old was his adulthood.

According to her best friend, she had shared with her they would have intercourse three times a day, every day, and this would explain how she came up pregnant and that produced the birth of a girl who came into this world with the name, Eva Geraldine.

By now, one would have thought that she would have settled into being Mrs. Dubbs, the perfect mother, and homemaker with the birth of Eva. However, she had other plans, and from time to time, the neighbors would notice her sneaking out of the house. One can only assume she was looking to having sex with whoever is available down at the Gin Mills. Unfortunately, when Dubbs finds out, she is sent packing to her mother. He keeps Eva with him, thinking it would bother her. However, it would have been something she'd been praying for; her freedom to pick up her old habit of seducing Brother Park; well, at least until her father brought Joe home, the new stud in town.

If things were not awful enough between them, Dubbs ran into Brother Park at a local tavern. For some unknown reason, Brother Park felt the need to tell Dubbs about his lifetime sexual relationship between him and his sister. Of course, this bit of news does not sit well with Dubbs, who now has vowed never to speak to Sylvia or Brother Park.

However, Brother Park was just causing trouble when he gets his rear end in an uproar over his sister's ongoing relationship with Joe. So he tells Joe that Sister was still married to Dubbs; something she had forgotten to mention; also forgetting to mention; Eva!

Yet, who knows, Eva may not have been Dubb's child. It could have been Brother Park's. However, Brother Park's news did not faze Joe one bit; he was so in love with Sylvia that his only concern was;

"When is she going to file for a divorce?"

One could find Joe perching himself on one or another fence rail around her yard, waiting until that day.

Right in the mitts of the love affair, Brother Park and Dubbs get drafted into the military. Brother Park is the first to leave home headed for basic training at Fort Hood, Texas. Dubbs followed him a few weeks later, born for his basic training at Fort Ord Military Base out in California. Now with Brother Park and Dubbs out of Sylvia's life, she is free to carry on her planned ardent love affair with Joe; and right in the middle of it, Joe gets his draft notice to report for basic training at Fort Sill, Oklahoma. During that time, Sylvia's other brothers joined the Marines. Her Sister Marylou is still living at home.

When Bill finishes his time in the Marines, he returns to Illinois, where he lives out life and worked as a Carpenter. He passes away in his eighties from a heart attack. Howard mustered out of the Marines in California, where remaining until his death. He became an electrician for the Bay Area Rapid Transit System in the San Francisco Bay Area and lived into his eighties before a heart attack took him. Ira also mustered out of the Marines in California and went to work in the San Francisco Bay Area in the Aero Space industry. Years later, he would retire and purchase a cattle ranch in Victor, Montana, and pass it on to natural causes at ninety-nine. When Brother Park gets out of the military and heads back home to Sterling, however, being the drifter winds up in the San Francisco Bay Area and takes the job of a house painter. In later years, he moves to Hollywood, Florida, where he lives in his late seventies before passing away due to liver failure. Marylou finished her schooling and eventually came to the San Francisco Bay Area, where she married a man named Harold who worked for the California Water District in Sacramento. She is the youngest to pass due to breast cancer in her late forties. Nora and Dennis left Sterling for Carson City, Nevada and then to Niles, California, where they went into the restaurant business. Years later, after closing the restaurant, they move onto Montana to help Ira on his cattle ranch. With Nora's failing health, she and Dennis leave Montana and move to Oroville, California, where Sylvia had migrated. Nora passes in her nineties because of a blood disorder. Dennis followed her eight years later of natural causes; he was ninety-nine.

After the birth of Eva, Sylvia vowed never to have another child even if she lived to be one hundred; however, that thought would change during the time she was dating Joe; Joe would not be the father. He had been married once before; however, they never had children.

With Dubb's long gone to War and Brother Park whipping his waddle in some shower in the men's lavatory each day down in Texas, tantalizing about his Sister, Joe becomes Sylvia's constant partner. Neither of them seemed to care who saw them together or where. From Sterling to Dixon to Clinton, anywhere there is a barn dance, a party, or a roadhouse. One could find them out behind a barn, parked outside behind an inn, or in some back room of a party house. Most men considered running as far as they could from Sylvia over her ways. She loved men, alcohol, smoking, and sex with any man who had the guts to do it to her after she had a few drinks. And the Scotch-Irish came tweaking out. Joe seemed to be the only man with guts enough to handle her.

Their whirlwind romance became interrupted when Nora and Dennis took a trip to visit Brother Park. Of course, Sylvia wanted to tag along but needed someone to care for Eva. Joe steps up as the perfect candidate. With that problem solved, the expedition departed for Texas. The Rock River's winter is still in February when they leave; however, where they were going in Texas would bring a warmer climate.

Upon arrival, the first thing was to hook up with Brother Park. That first night Nora and Dennis retire early while Sylvia and Brother Park head out barhopping. At one bar, Brother Park introduces Sylvia to another soldier named Francesco Stallone. Francesco had come into the Army from Maryland, or maybe it was New York, where he had been or was trying to be a hairstylist. It's not known how he gets into the arm forces being from Gioia del Colle in Puglia, Italy.

Sylvia wasted no time getting into her new friend's pants. And like two Possums, there they were out in the middle of some tall prairie grass along the roadside next to a music nightspot humping into the wind until some climax is achieved. For the next remaining weeks, these two remain inseparable until it is time for Sylvia and her family to return home.

Having sex with Francesco was not probably the best decision that Sylvia could have made, considering he was shipping out in seventy-two hours, heading for a war zone to free the French. However, it's a done deed, and the family now heads back home to the tranquility of Sterling.

Sylvia misses her subsequent two periods and knows it is her body's way of telling her she is indeed pregnant; her symptoms were the same when she is pregnant with Eva; this puts her in a dilemma every thought now is to find Francesco. However, where would one look? By far, he was deep into Europe, and the Army was not giving up that information.

Sylvia had no other choice other than to turn to her cunning ways. Without Mr. Stallone, she needs to find a substitute replacement; the only name to enter her head is, of course, Joe. However, to snag him, she would need a plan of action, and she is going to have to work fast if she is to pull it off before he's leaving for the Army within days; her intention is not only to get him into bed; but getting him to marry her before he left.

Unfortunately, time is not on her side; Joe leaves earlier than expected. Her plan would have been, after they marry, to wait a month before pronouncing him a Father. With him going soon, she is now in a real fix; if the town folk ever found out; this would bring shame down on her and not mention the devastation it will bring upon her family. She is not one to give up, and she came up with another plan; to head for the nearest bar where she will find a few Fathers.

Her luck was holding court that day. Before she put her plan into action, Joe calls and tells her the Army had discharged him because his legs keep swelling over his boots during boot camp training; not only is he coming home, while he has her on the phone, he proposes marriage. She does not even try to be coy and says, yes.

Of course, she made a vow to leave Joe right after the Bastard child she is, carrying is, born. Unfortunately for her, she needed to wait out those long upcoming months. When that day arrives, she had already contrived a story to tell Joe that her newborn was premature. Of course, it is a secret to her that the baby she is carrying took a full nine months.

On the day of my birth, Joe, Sylvia, and Eva lived in an apartment just above the town's drugstore. Sylvia is lying on the bed suffering the complications of labor pains; they were coming quicker and quicker and getting more severe than they had been an hour before. Then it is time, and with Nora acting as midwife, she hurries to her expecting daughter, bringing warm water and towels, just in time to hear Sylvia say,

"It is coming; the Bastard is coming."

Right then, I started fighting my way out of what had been one hell hole; with assurances, through the light coming on the other side, there is another hell waiting. In agony, Sylvia grabs hold of the sides of the mattress, as the pains of birth gained its momentum; she is trying to keep her thoughts somewhere else, like the sound of thunder rolling across the dark sky outside and crashing down on the windowpanes. However, her thoughts were interrupted by another sound louder than the storm outside; it's the sound of me. I weigh in at nine-pounds-two-ounces and arrived into the world on a cold, blustery morning at 10:31 am.

At first sight, Joe immediately wanted to name me "Tiger," a name he used during his pro fighting days. Of course, Dennis put in his two cents. He wanted to name me "Digger," after some radio program called "Digger O'Dell the Friendly Undertaker" however, Nora spoke up, and she decides on the name Rocky; my mother sided with grandmother.

Life in the river city continued; World War II ends. War-torn European countries rebuild by using Steel produced in their own countries instead of Steel made in the

United States, causing Northwestern to relinquish cutbacks, and several men get ended; Joe became one of them.

These days, the daily topic around the family household is finding work. From a friend of father's who had just returned from vacationing in the State of Nevada, he brings the news that becomes life-changing when he said,

"The Carson City Brewing Company in Carson City, Nevada is hiring truck drivers."

Father thought,

"Nevada! That is sure a far distance from Sterling, and there is no workaround here that it might be worth going out there while I still have the money to make such a trip."

He makes a long-distance call to the Brewery, and as his friend had stated, they required drivers. However, he would need to get out to them right away. He discussed the idea with mother, and it is, decided he would go out to Carson City first, secure the job, and then send for her and Eva, and me. Deep with her thoughts, she is thrilled to think she's getting free of him; and with her blessing, he's boarding a bus headed for the Train Station in Chicago where he will catch the westbound to Carson, City.

Leaving Sterling, the exhaust smoke from the bus had barely dissipated before mother heads for the nearest Tavern. Of course, Eva and I were deposited over with our Grandparents. She continued her partying for another year until the town is once again deep in winter. Father, who is now calling himself Bob, called to say he is ready to have his family depart on their western journey. However, with Grandmother being in poor health, there is no way mother is leaving her behind. Ironically, the very day that he calls, Grandmother's Doctor has diagnosed her with having Acute Myelogenous Leukemia. I.e., cancer that causes constitutional changes in the blood cells that produce granulocytes, a type of white blood cells made in the bone marrow called blasts that cannot mature. Her Doctor felt a drier climate might lengthen her life; suppose one could consider mother as a wildflower. However, for sure, she loved her mother and told my father of her mother's health problem and that she would only agree to the trip as long as her parents were to come. Was it is fate or just totally unplanned that Dennis had a relative living fifty miles to the east of Carson City, in the hamlet of Fallon. Grandfather contacted his relative, and with their blessing for a safe trip, it was agreed my Grandparents would go out to Nevada.

On the day of the planned trip, I have turned a year old. On that day, while everyone is preparing to travel, a blizzard is beating down mercilessly along the river community, turning the sky into a miserable gray as the streets themselves became entrenched in inches of the powdery snow, causing them to be almost treacherous. Those asphalt potholes of plenty had now filled with packed snow, and the small river town is at its usual snarl.

Despite the conditions, my Grandparents and Eva had made it over to our apartment. However, as usual, mother is still preparing for the trip. Everyone is seated in the front room, waiting for her to shower, put on her makeup, and dress. When she is ready, we all stepped out into the blizzard of the century. Mother took the lead, with my Grandparents being next, followed by Eva, who held me as we worked our way down through the space between the buildings to the street. Grandfather hailed a taxi to take us to the bus station that will take us to the train station in Chicago.

Chapter 2: Exodus

After hours of riding, the bus driver's voice comes over the intercom.

"We're here, folks!"

It is a welcoming sound for everyone.

Grandfather replied, "Good thing, was about to call off the trip, but there is no way we want to travel back over those roads again this day."

No sooner had we entered the massive Station, we immediately smell the odor of train oil, the dust, and the smoke-filled air that added to our trip even more real. Leaving town during any early winter is not a familiar experience for any of us. Except for me, there is a sense of going away from a very ordinary town, one they would never really know again. Of course, my Grandparents had mixed feelings, with added thoughts for what they were giving up and the excitement of what might lie ahead.

The late afternoon sky is still a blur of whirling snow as we all boarded the Westbound Train with Grandmother, not too pleased with all the noise and confusion surrounding the train station, the urgency and rudeness of people all around her. Then there was my mother's attitude to contend with, as she felt being forced to go west. If she had it her way, she would just as well have stayed home where the good time boys lived.

Despite her attitude, the Train departed out of the Station. The grownups knew they were on their way to a new life's adventure and were made sure of it while looking out of the Train's windows and seeing familiar landmarks that symbolized that they were leaving their past behind and giving their thoughts of what lies ahead.

As the Train continued into the State of Iowa, darkness had fallen. Eve was sitting next to me, while staring out the window into the darkness of the snowy night, looking for the occasional flash of light from some far-off town. My Grandparents had an edgy look upon their faces now that the Train had pulled out of the Station. Mother found a soldier returning from the War, and she had all but forgotten about the rest of us.

The days on the Train were long, as were the nights, as the enormous steam engine continued its winding path across America. When arriving in Reno, we switched trains heading for Carson City. At the Carson City Station, father was waiting out on the wooden platform like a faithful Spaniel. The first to get off the Train was Eva and then my grandparents with grandmother holding me, followed by mother. Upon seeing father, mother walked up to him and gave him a peck on the lips, as if to say.

"I'm here, now what ass whole?"

Because my father is so much in love with her, he did not notice her snobbish attitude; he just reached down and picked up what suitcases he could carry while the rest of us followed him, heading for the car. As soon as the luggage was loaded and everyone seated, we were off down the road for the fifty-mile ride into Fallon to drop off my grandparents so they could start their new jobs; her being the cook and he the groundskeeper. With them safely there, father turned the car around and heads towards Carson City, where he has rented a house.

Mother only made it three months before she's bound, determined to find herself a lover besides father. She plans for every detail of her upcoming adventure and waits for the right time when father works late, and that day finally comes. She knew father was on his scheduled monthly beer run; the run would take him to several towns that he did not serve during the rest of the month, which meant he would work overtime.

She dresses and feeds me, and then puts me into my bed, then leaves the house. She knew father's last run was in Reno, only thirty miles from Carson City, and he should not be that late in getting home. Usually, he came back every night simultaneously; however, this night, he would be much later, and of all nights, I am left alone this night. One might suggest that it was my first experience with child neglect; however, it would not be my last.

Mother had not considered the winter storm that was making the roads covered with packed snow. Indeed, the snow had been falling most of the day, and father's route had taken him east through Dayton, Silver Springs, and on into Fallon. He headed north over the mountain passes to reach the town of Fernley; from there, he headed west to the city of Reno before turning South headed back to the Brewery.

Despite the blizzard conditions, he had made his last Reno stop and was heading towards home. He is on Road 395, heading south when he runs into a roadblock, and where a Nevada State Highway Patrol Trooper was standing in the middle of the road.

"Sir, I am afraid you will need to turn around. I'd advise you against trying to get through Washoe tonight."

The road through Washoe Valley followed the shoreline around Washoe Lake.

Trooper, "Even if you did somehow make it through, you still have the 5200-foot climb over Lakeview Summit to get to Carson City on the other side."

Father refuses to listen to the Trooper and heads for the summit. He made it around the lake. However, it is when he's halfway up the mountain that does him in, sure enough, that Trooper was right, and he finds himself stranded. It is not until past midnight before a farmer with his tractor came along and pulled him and his rig over to the other side.

Now he's very late in getting home, so he does not even bother to return his delivery truck; his excitement is to get home to mother and to explain why he is so late. He worries about her being concerned about his whereabouts. He just knew how worried she must be (not), and he was kicking himself for refusing to put a telephone in the house.

When he arrives, he jumps running from the truck and heads straight for the house front door, which he finds left wide-open. Once inside, he calls out for mother and gets no answer. He continues searching through the entire home only to find it empty, which gets him thinking,

"She and Rocky must be over at the neighbor's."

Apparently, I had gotten out of my bed, walked to the front porch, then down three-level steps into the snow covering the yard and kept walking until I am forced to stop when a tree branch snapped and come falling down on me; I was going over to the neighbor's house. There I was stuck with only one thing to do; slowly freeze.

As father is crossing the yard, he trips over me, and it causes him to roll down the slight embankment that was on the other side of where I was turning into freezer material. He climbs back up the slippery snow and goes looking for what caused him to trip. That's when he sees what looked like a half-frozen dog with a tree branch covering it; however, by striking a match, upon further inspection, he sees it's me under that branch, half-frozen.

"What the hell," is what he is thinking?

He removed the branch and picked me up with trembling hands, then rushed me to the truck and placed me in the cab where the heater is still warm; after a few minutes of rubbing, I warm up. With some assurance, I will not die; he leaves me on the truck seat while he goes to check with the neighbors in the wee hours to see if they might know the whereabouts of mother.

After waking up in the neighborhood, he learns no one has seen her. As he walked back to the truck, his temper is rising; he may have loved her. However, he was a hot-headed Italian who did not like being played like a fool. After seeing me lying there in the snow, he did not doubt that she was up to no good, and he vows to find her.

However, first I needed a safe and dry place before any search could take place, and he drives through the snowy night out on Highway 50 to the ranch in Fallon, and there he leaves me with my grandparents.

On his way back towards Carson City, he checked the Tavern in Silver Springs, and when he does not find her there, he continues to the town of Dayton. When he walks into that Tavern, he sees mother sitting over at a corner table with two other men; the three laugh and have a big time as the angry father approached. Here is a man six feet three and weighing in at two hundred and seventy-five pounds; getting him mad is somewhat like waking up a sleeping giant.

The closer he gets, the more furious he becomes. Reaching their table, he comes to a stop and then, without saying a word, reaches out and grabs a hand full of hair and then pulls the man up and out of his chair, over the table past mother, and right into the other man's lap. He then takes one look at her and then calls her a bitch, before turning around and walking out of the Tavern. He never mentions to her where he had found me; he just turned away from her and her two scared companions and headed back to his truck. As he is driving off, she comes running out of the Tavern, but not in time to stop him from driving away and returning to the ranch to tell my Grandmother,

"No woman is going to play me; you know I've been thinking for some time about moving to California, and I can't find any better time than the present."

He mentioned where he found Mother, yet he gives no details. When he left the ranch that night, he never considers my welfare; he just said his goodbyes to my grandparents and headed out the door. He returned to the

Carson City Brewery to drop off his delivery truck and pick up his car, and then he makes a stop by his house and packs what he needs for the trip, then loads his car and starts for California.

His destination is the town of Niles; however, he had to drive over Donner Summit and the snow-packed Sierra Nevada Mountains. For some time, he has heard rumors of a steel mill in Niles, California called "Pacific States Steel," and it needed skillful steelworkers. For the production of Steel, father was the best.

Niles California, during its earlier years, was the home of Essanay Studios. Many first films were produced there, including most of "Bronco Billy" Anderson's westerns. The most famous films were those starring Charlie Chaplin. It is in Niles where Chaplin's "Little Tramp" character first appeared.

The town's train depot had seen several other famous and not-so-famous stars arriving and leaving. However, the city is compact with a Main Street, and two others are known as Second and Third; it is one of California's most visited spots of its day.

The Pacific States Steel Corporation and its neighbor, the Crystal Company, were in Union City, out on the Niles Alvarado Road, and both corporations were significant employers in the area along with Gallerson's Gravel Pit.

When father arrived in town, his first choice to stop to ask directions was "Joe's Corner Soda Parlor and Billiard Room" on the corner of Main and J. Street. With instructions got, he leaves Joe's Corner and heads out on the Niles Alvarado Road. After locating the Mill, he pulled into the parking lot, found a parking place, and then headed for the hiring office. When making Steel, father held the title of Heater Helper, a very hard person to find back in the day.

When he leaves the Mill that day, he had secured a job, and now his new challenge is to find living quarters. He searched for a better part of his day, looking all around Niles. However, he finds nothing. He returns to Joe's Corner, asking the patrons if they knew of a place to stay, and learns of Pleasanton. It is about ten miles via what the locals referred to as Niles Canyon, and after getting directions, he's off driving through the Canyon, and when he arrives in Pleasanton, he starts his search and locates a small cottage.

Within a few days taken to settle into his new surroundings, he makes a call to my grandmother, letting her know where he is living and the job he had. Within a month of that call, one day, when his shift ended, he's headed for the parking lot, and when he is within the eyesight of his car, he noticed someone was standing by it. The closer he came to the vehicle, the clearer the people became; it was me, with mother. His first thoughts were to play it coy until mother started begging him to forgive her. And of course, no one ever said father wasn't madly in love with her. Without showing his excitement, he takes her back.

It did not take mother long to get back into her rotten ways. Right off, the town of Pleasanton became too small, especially after having sex with every available man. She talks Father into moving into a trailer park, miles away in the bay area town of Castro Valley. Then, no sooner had we settled in did my grandparents show up when they brought Eva home. They had left the ranch with plans to start up a new venture. What luck, the mobile home right next door is for rent?

My grandparents had barely gotten settled in when one afternoon they drove over to Niles. Father had mentioned to them that there is a restaurant and gasoline station for sale on Main Street with an attached mechanic's garage to the Station.

For them came another bit of luck; if they purchased the property, right across the street is the town's only theater, and above it was an apartment for rent. After meeting with the realtor and the rental agent, they purchased the restaurant property and rented the apartment. After three months of remodeling, the restaurant opens under the name Candlelight Café, the only Café around for several miles.

The community supported several Companies that produced steel, bricks, chemicals, a rock quarry, all operating twenty-four hours a day. It causes the Café also to remain open twenty-four-hour a day, serving the workers. My grandparents realized their Café would never be an eight-hour restaurant. After the first year, grandmother started baking fruit pies, and that grew into a major factory. People would come to the restaurant from all ends of the earth to purchase one of her Pies.

Father leased the Station from grandfather, and it too became a twenty-four-hour service station. Since he opened, he started a used car lot on the dirt lot next to the theater. With the money father and mother were making working in Niles, they purchased twenty acres in the small rural farm community south of Hayward known as Valle Vista; he intended to start an auto salvage yard. However, he had forgotten whom he married.

I had never seen my father as happy as he was living out in the country. Of course, mother was not happy living there and learning from her mother that her brother Howard was moving out of Illinois. She sees her way out of the farm by getting Howard to purchase it. With her mindset, she complains daily about the place and finally convinces father to sell it to Howard.

It meant we would need another place to live with that sale, somewhere that had plenty of beer joints for mother. However, father moved us to a town that did not fit her way of thinking at all. He rented a two-bedroom Spanish Stucco on Second Street in Niles. Of course, living there is boring for mother until she finds that over her backyard fence is Joe's Corner Soda Parlor and Billiard Room, a place where just about every worker in the area hung out who is coming and going to work. Unbeknownst to father, her daily ritual is to sneak through the broken boards in the backyard fence on a quest for sex while leaving me at home with Eva. Of course, by now, father had not the time to watch a wife because he had become a workaholic. When he was not working at the Mill, he had the Station, and for something more to do, he had the car lot.

Aunt Marylou shows up in Niles; what a beautiful woman she was; the kind men have killed over; her beauty was what one supposed the word Goddess came. She moved in with her parents and where Eva had now chosen to live. She works at the restaurant alongside mother, who had given up on Joe's Corner and worked on the men who came into the Candlelight Cafe. There is not a day that goes by where some man would ask Marylou out on a date. When she took them up on their offer, he must bring a friend along for her sister, who is a Goddess in her own right. Mother continued her cheating on father every chance she got. I am no problem since I spend most of my time over at my grandparents.

I am still living in Niles when I reach the age to enroll in school. I am six years old when I start Kindergarten at Niles Elementary. Eva would walk me there every day since she too attended there. Eva had taken going there for two more years. I attended my second and third grades at Centerville Elementary, in Centerville, where father had moved us after purchasing a home. Eva remained living with our grandparents in Niles.

The home he had purchased was on Pine Street. It is while living there that I had gotten myself into trouble when mother caught me using a hammer out on the rear stoop, trying to set off twenty-two caliber rifle bullets. We lived in the house for six months before father sold it and built a home in Glenmoore Gardens, the newest housing development in Centerville.

The new home is the second one constructed on the housing development property. It sat right on a corner lot, and what a beauty it was. When most houses in the day only had a one-car garage, this one had a double one. Inside the house, four bedrooms, four baths, and on the outside, the entire fenced yard surrounding the house had climbed roses planted all along it. The grass was bright green and plush, with Chinese hedges lining its walkways. The house was father's new dream home; of course, mother could have cared less; she was now courting a new beau behind his back.

Cal was the name he gave that early afternoon when he came into the Candlelight Café; Mother and Aunt Marylou had just finished serving the lunch hour. Cal sits down at the luncheonette counter and its mother, who took his order,

"Blue Plate Special Please,"

Pork Chops, Mash Potatoes, and a Veggie of the day. Cal told mother that he was a musician who is singing over at the Garden of Alai Nightclub, out on Highway 238. Before he left that day, he invited the sisters to come and hear him.

Cal was eleven years younger than mother and pleasant to look at; about five feet five inches tall, and the girls jumped at his offer. The one night, turns into another, and then another until Cal has run off with mother, one piece at a time if one gets my meaning. Because of mother's indiscretions, it caused me in the future to have spent a night outside alone.

My School Bus had dropped me off; I headed straight for my house. I ran up to the front door, and upon trying to open it, I found it locked. I thought that to be unusual. However, to occupy me, I hung out in the backyard playing with my yard toys lying around, and by nightfall, no one has come home.

Directly across the street from the house was a Walnut Orchard with an excellent loading platform built on the site for workers to put their filled boxes of Walnuts in waiting for pickup. I head for the platform with nothing to do, knowing from there I could monitor the house should someone come home; within minutes, I had all but forgotten

I was locked out because I was acting like some fool jumping and dancing around the platform. An hour passes, and out of a clear sky, it started raining; it wasn't the average rainfall; it was a flash flood, and I am caught right in its downpour. My first thought was to run under a walnut tree branch that was hanging over the platform. The rain kept falling, and soon the orchard floor was becoming puddles of water, leaving me no other choice other than to stay right where I was.

I was already fighting off a cold and now here I am, soaked through. And it did not help matters that nightfall had to arrive, and that was terrifying. The only thought I had going for me was wishing someone would come home and save me. However, that was not happening, and the night was at its darkest.

That morning I should have stayed home, especially having a fever. However, the rain could have cared less about how I felt and continued pouring down. It was past midnight, and with the tree leaves talking to me, the more terrified I become, then the thought came to me.

"If I cried my heart out, would it somehow make it all go away?"

Then I wondered,

"Has any other seven-year-old been left deserted and cold, and soaked to the bone and hungry? Would they be afraid?"

Here I am out there alone with that awful lightning trying to get me. Should I even think of running to the house, which that thought alone was an impossibility because the only place with any cover was a small front porch overhang. The wind and rain would not let up.

I am getting the shakes, and exhaustion sets in as the elements take their toll to worsen matters. Finally, I dropped to the platform puddles and by using my hands as an umbrella; I covered my face as the hard, pouring rain took its course with me. The wind was turning colder, and as the water poured down, I started shivering terribly. I am so tired and wishing everything would stop. However, with nothing to cover me, I continue shivering. After a while, I felt exhausted from crying, from hunger, and the feeling of being, I'm forgotten, and now comes even a higher fever, that at least caused sleep to come over me as I am laying in that rain-drenched nightmare.

As the earth turned into the morning sun, father finally comes home after being out all night looking for mother. He gets out of his car and heads for the front door when he hears me.

"Help me, please help me."

He heard me asking for help and started looking around where the sound came from, his first thought.

"It's coming from over at the Walnut Orchard."

He goes towards the sound, and upon reaching the platform, he sees me motionless, lying there. He jumps up on the platform and assures me he's there, and upon further inspection, he's checking my faint pulse as I am lying there with my eyes opened as the rain is still not letting up as it continues pouring down on my face. A horrified look came across father's face as it had once before when he found me in the snow, freezing. He picked me up and carried me to the car, and then sped off to the hospital. The attending physician, upon inspection, said,

"Besides a fever, I fear pneumonia has set in, but I feel the boy will pull through. It's a good thing that you found him when you did."

Short of a miracle that I pulled through, however, when I opened my eyes and the first person I see is father sitting over in a chair. Seeing movement, he gets up and comes across to the bedside; as he reached out for my hand, I pulled it back.

Instead of asking about my condition, he was more concerned about whether I had any knowledge of the war bouts of my mother; from that day forward, I had no use for my mother or father.

After being released from the hospital, I never saw the Centerville home again. My father places me with my Uncle Howard and as for Cal and Mother; they continued their lovers' plight across America as Cal played his music from one nightclub after another.

When my father finally realizes, mother is not coming back; he borrows a camp trailer from my Uncle Howard and pulls it to Reno, Nevada. There, he files for a divorce. He remained living in the camp trailer as a Nevada residence for six weeks; one must be a resident for not less than six weeks to make a divorce official. With that divorce degree in hand, he heads back to California, only to get into a wreck and in doing so, the camp trailer gets damaged.

Now that he's divorced, he sells the Centerville home, turns the gasoline station over to grandfather, closes out the used-car business, and moves to a Cottage sitting on Uncle Howard's property. One would have thought that he wanted to move there because I am living there. However, that was not the case; he only moved there because he would have an acre of land where he could repair the trailer.

If having morons for parents was not enough, I had become the family's pivot point for all their gossip. Like the day when the hell's fury came around when Uncle Howard tells father what my Uncle Park had told him years before, and that was.

Uncle Howard, "Well, Bob, I have been holding something from you for some time, and I want to clear my conscience."

Father replied, "What might that be, Howard?"

Uncle Howard, "It concerns what Park had to say just after Rocky was born. He told me you were not Rocky's father. One of his Army buddies named Francesco Stallone is."

Father replied, "You're nuts. You cannot believe anything Park says."

Father thought the man was undoubtedly jesting; however, he knew Howard was not the person to tell such a lie. However, what had been said got father to wonder? Of course, this news came as a total shock and as the days pass, the more he gets to thinking about what Howard had to say, and the more furious he becomes. He felt it is just another of the many knives mother had already planted on his back. With hearing I am not his biological son and thought,

"If only I had learned of this before I filed for divorce, I would not have asked for custody of Rocky."

What happens now is father becomes much colder towards me. That is funny if one considers I could have cared less what my father thought or did. His actions were not anything I could not have guessed would happen, especially coming from such a dysfunctional man and his shenanigans.

Even at my young age, I could see everything about my father and mother was abnormal as could be and had been from the day I have been old enough to understand my surroundings. If any good coming out of what my Uncle Howard had to say is; I jumped with joy upon hearing whom I thought my father isn't. My only concern I wanted to meet my biological father. In the meantime, the most beneficial news is I would not be obliged to worry about freezing in a bank of snow or being locked out of the house on a stormy night by a man who is so enthralled with my mother that he had no concern for whom at the time he thought was his son left alone at home.

Life somewhat settles down at Uncle Howard's house between father and me; neither one of us was having anything to do with the other. Then, as sure as Stink comes from crap, Cal and Mother return to Niles from where who knows and moves in with my grandparents. Joining their gypsy caravan is a child they referred to as Melvin, who turns out to be my first, yet not the last, half-brother.

It does not take mother long before she shows up at Uncle Howard's on her quest to get her oldest son, me, to come and live with her and Cal. Of course, I knew my mother enough to know that she had something other on her mind. I figured she most likely needed a babysitter for Melvin or the money father would pay her to keep me.

Uncle Howard had no problem with her request. However, he suggested that since father was my legal guardian; she needed to discuss the move with him. Of course, father would not have cared where I lived; he is not having anything to do with me.

Facing off with father was not a problem for mother, not at all; there was no shame in that soul. She heads around to the side of the barn, where father was remodeling the damaged camper and confronts him. The first words to come out of his mouth are,

"I want to know Sylvia. Is Rocky my son or not?"

Mother, "What kind of question is that. Don't be more unintelligent than you already are. Of course, he is your child. Who else's would he be? For Christ's sake, you of all people know I had always been faithful to you until Cal."

I overheard what she had to say, and I wondered if my hearing was going.

"Did she say faithful; she can't even spell the word?"

Unintelligent does what unintelligent does, and now father has fallen for what she had to say. Of course, mother's way of thinking was if the man was foolish to have married her in the first place, he would believe anything she said and that always worked to her advantage. When she got through with him, he was not only convinced he had been lied to by Uncle Howard, and therefore he would not stay on the same property with someone who would lie like that?

Father continued working on the camp trailer the rest of that day with a smile on his face, while singing praises that mother had always been faithful to him. As for mother, had she forgotten about the multiples of men she already seduced? Unfortunately for me, I am back on being Father's son. He instantly found this new passion for me, who by now had become the most wonderful son that any man could ever have; I could hardly wait for the next stormy night.

What father did not let out of the bag; after what Uncle Howard had told him, he's determined to be excommunicated from being my designated guardian. He went back to Reno to get that changed, only to be recognized by the divorce judge that nothing could be done about it. He suggested to father that he could find another person to take his place or stay the sole guardian until I turned eighteen. Now, with what mother had to say, father is more than happy to let his wonderful son live with his faithful mother, never mind asking me if even I wanted to do so.

With the car loaded with my things, I am headed for Niles. The only change in the living department was they had moved out of my grandparent's house to their own on North Second Street.

Chapter 3: Angus and Alma

Living with Cal and Mother comprised attending school, coming home to pick up beer bottles, emptying ashtrays, and trying to straighten up the house around two drunks, and then babysitting Melvin; occasionally mother, when sober, would cook dinner. Usually, Melvin and I would walk to the Candlelight Cafe, where grandmother would feed us; otherwise, most of the time, we would have gone with nothing in our bellies. However, you could bet my kindness never went without a reward from Cal.

Because I would take Melvin with me to the restaurant, usually when we returned, Cal would make me spend the rest of my evening in my room locked in the closet, while pampering a busted lip or some bump on my head from a beer bottle. It got so I would have Melvin meet me in the middle of the block from our house. Upon returning, I would see that Melvin got in the door. However, I would head down the street to my best friend, Poncho; the two of us would run amuck through the streets late at night. In time, I had moved over to Poncho's house.

Because of Cal, I made a pack within myself to stay over at Poncho's or with my grandparents, leaving them to their lifestyle of alcohol. The problem was, Cal was jealous of me, being my father's son. Just the thought of mother once having had sex with father would drive him crazy, especially when he got drunk. I certainly would not stay in a home with the likes of Cal. I never liked his abusiveness and slapping me across my head with beer bottles every chance and being locked in my room for days without food or water. Cal would do his best in trying to prove to her he is a bigger man; his problem was his thinking; he could not distinguish the difference between me, not being, my father.

One would have thought he could see the difference in ages. However, what could one expect from a man who was a drunk?

I finally made a life running throughout the streets of Niles. It was in the alleys behind the Merchants stores on Main Street, where Poncho and I made most of our spending money. The merchants would store all their returnable beer and soda bottles in a fenced area out back of their establishments next to the alley. It was not any problem for us to jump the wooden fences and steal their returnable bottles. The next day at first light, with our wagon loaded, we would pull it to where we had gotten the bottles in the first place and return them for the deposit. Sometimes, we would jump the fence of the local grocer stealing their bottles, and the next day; there we were inside collecting deposits.

In my life now, the meaning of child abuse has been planted deep within, and now it is time for sexual exploitation. Life is taking on a familiar tone for abuse from my peers, beginning with Cal. At my age, anything and everything I see or experienced stays within my thoughts, and some things I encountered, has stayed with me a lifetime. There are the likes of Angus, and he was a fifty-something-year-old schoolteacher who lived in a rooming house above the Pontiac Dealership on the corner of Main and G Streets. That building was, initially, constructed as a Motion Picture Studio. When the industry moved to Las Angeles, the building is remodeled, and the second floor is turned into rooms to rent.

Angus usually took his meals at the Candlelight Cafe. He was the type of man who always needed a shave, and a good bath now and then would have undoubtedly helped his overall appearance; he would get around town on a Cushman Motor Scooter, and there were many times when he would give me rides around the hamlet. On one particular afternoon, as I am walking down the sidewalk on Main Street, he pulls up to the curb and invites me to go for a ride over to the town of Centerville. I had nothing better to do, so I accepted his offer. By mid-afternoon, we had covered every street in Centerville and started back for Niles. Halfway home, Angus pulls into a gasoline station because both of us needed to relieve ourselves. Once inside, I headed for the stall while Angus used the wall urinal. When I finished my business, as I pulled up my zipper, Angus came barging in and shoved me up against the stall. He wasted no time reaching for my crouch while saying,

"I am going to suck your penis, and if you don't let me, I will break your neck and leave you here to die."

Of course, I am terrified of thinking he might kill me, especially with being pinned down and having his arm around my neck while maneuvering around, trying to get my pants undone. When Angus finally got to my penis, he got on his knees and sucked until I climaxed. He then turned me around and tried everything he could think of to put his penis up inside of me, and everything he tried failed. When he tried to put his penis in, I tighten my muscles. His alternative was to masturbate and coming all over my butt. When finished, he said to me,

"I sure wish you had a little more penis."

I told him,

"One day Angus. Just wait."

He never questioned my comeback answer; he was more concerned that I might tell someone what he had just done and said.

"Pull up your pants, and boy, never think of telling anyone, or I will kill you for real. Are we clear on this?"

"It's kind of late for you to be worrying, don't you think?"

We continued the ride into Niles, and every so often, Angus would pull over to the side of the road to assure he had made his point about me not saying anything about what had happened. Unfortunately for Angus, I did not enjoy people trying to put things up inside me.

Once I was back in Niles and safely away from Angus, I went to the Candlelight Café and ran into Cal. Being stupid, I told him about what Angus had done. However, that opened Pandora's Box. He immediately took me to confront the man. When we arrived at his apartment door, Cal tells me.

"Boy, you stay put here in the hallway while I go inside to talk with this guy.

Within minutes, Cal is back and said.

"He has given me two-hundred dollars and his Cushman Scooter. So, listen up, kid, you don't tell anyone what has taken place here; if you do!"

Despite Cal and Angus, life in Niles continued with Poncho and I jumping the alley fences and then there came the day when we entered one Tavern and I notice Angus sitting over at a corner table, and as soon as he sees me, he immediately leaves.

At that bar were sitting these two men who were, strangely enough, discussing him, saying he's been taking young boys to his hotel room across the street from the Tavern and paying them ten dollars to have oral and anal sex. Hearing what the men were talking about, Poncho just had to tell them of my experience. And of course, their conversation leads to the men wanting Poncho to set up Angus because he had not met him before. The only question, which I could not get an answer to, is why these men wanted to set up Angus? Poncho went over to the hotel and knocked on the door. When Angus answered, Poncho said.

"I came here because another boy said you would pay me money for sex."

Of course, Angus never realizes he is being set up, invites Poncho in, pays him ten dollars, and tells him to undress and get on the bed. The two men waiting out in the hallway could hear the entire conversation, and when they overhear Angus telling Poncho,

"I can't wait to taste you."

The two men broke into the room, and it did not take them long before Poncho and I were running straight out of the hotel and as fast as we could.

The next day, the buzz about town is about Angus and how the hotel management found him in his room, with his arms tied to the bedpost; they were severed from his body. His legs were, roped to the end board. His torso is on the floor alongside the bed without its head. It is not until days later before anyone finds it. It was in the Alameda

Creek with Angus's penis stuck in its mouth. It would be another time when we would see those men again. Neither Poncho nor I ever knew those men before that day. However, as far as I was concerned, revenge is sweet, and Angus got more than he could have hoped.

I had often wondered if there were such entities known as heaven and God, and if so, why was I sent to earth just to be continually punished. So far, for being so young, many unexpected events had come my way, like when my father shows up at mothers suggesting he not be made to pay her for my support while I am living with her and Cal. After all, she requested I come and live with her.

After my father comes for a visit, it is only another few weeks more before I am packing again. To me; the only reason Cal tolerated me at all is for the money father was paying. Without that money coming in, Cal had this need to get rid of me. Of course, he did not want father to think the money issue, is the reason. Therefore, Cal comes up with the perfect plan, to mention the Angus affair, hoping father might think that mother was incompetent in raising his son and removes me from their home.

Cal's plan worked, and father took me to live with my Uncle Howard again and would forever consider me to be some gay bastard; his words, not mine. After I moved out, for whatever the reason, Cal moved his family to Northlake, Illinois, where mother's brother Bill and his wife Mary lived. Cal stopped playing music and took a job as a factory worker. They rented the top floor inside Bill and Mary's home.

With recent events that have caused father to have a problem with thinking he had a gay son, he moves out of the Cottage at Howard's and moves five miles up the road in Hayward. It would be a rare moment for him to come and visit me.

His attention now is given to the woman who came into his life; her name was Alma. They met at the Cazbar on Main Street in Hayward. After mustering out of the Army, she had come to America from England as a Master Drill Sergeant. If there is one thought embedded in her brain, it was the idea that others could do what they wished for their own lives, as long as they asked her first. She had gotten to America via her Spanish husband Rudy, whom she met while the two were in the military. He was in the United States Army, and she was in the service of her Queen. Both were, stationed in Cairo, Egypt, during World War II. She had only married Rudy because of her need for a sponsor, enabling her to live in America. However, within months of their arrival, they divorced. For her to stay in the country, she would need to find another sponsor. She found one in my father, and sure enough, he marries her.

I had grown older now, and because of all the abuse I had to take from my family members, I spend most of my days now as a serious boy and one who had learned he would not take any more crap from the likes of Father, Howard, or Cal. God help any other man wanting to touch my body.

A year into Father and Alma's marriage, Howard shows up at their door because he felt, since my father was my guardian, it would be better if I came to live with him. His aim reasoning for such action stemmed from me telling him what father thought about him after lying to him about me not being his son, a little revenge from me that is gowning to backfire on me

I moving in with my Father and Alma was like saying Satan is moving in. Over the years of spending most of my time living out in the streets, I had become street smart. I was dead set on hating Alma. The way I figured, it is best to hate her before she becomes like Cal. I knew for sure as the nose is upon my face that Alma would reject me for no other reason than being my mother's son. I was entering a home where Alma is jealous of my mother for having been married to my father once upon a time. I could not get a break if my life depended on it. With Cal, it was no different; the exception was his jealousy over mother having sex with my father; living with that jealousy alone was going to be torture enough.

Of course, it did not help me be better looking than all of them, including my Mother and Aunt Marylou combined; because of Alma's jealousy and my good looks, I could see right away she was out to make me pay for forever being born by what she had to say the first two minutes of me walked into the house; as she once put it,

"I'll tell you what, you fagot, before I am through with you, I'm going to wipe your good looks right off your fricking face."

She hated children. Her reasoning stemmed from when she is twelve. A cousin of hers hit her below her stomach so hard with his fist that it damaged something, causing her never to have children; because she could not have her own, she most likely gained her hatred for other kids.

Right out of the gate on my first day is when she started giving me her many orders, like standing there at attention when she is confronting me. Awaken every day at five and making my bed so a coin could be, bounced on it, taking a bath, brushing the teeth, and combing my hair, then standing at attention for inspection.

My inspections were exciting and comprised checking the inside of my mouth, looking under my armpits. When she was done, she allowed me to report to the kitchen for my daily breakfast of dry toast with a glass of water. Then I was off for kitchen duty, washing not only my plate and drinking glass but also the breakfast dishes that my father would leave every day at three in the morning before heading to work. After the kitchen was clean, I am outside to pick weeds out of the yard, and my last chore was to take out the garbage. Then and only then was I allowed to go to school; I had to run to get there before the last bell rang. God help me should I ever mess up on any of my chores or did something she did not like; there was a punishment for that.

Our house sat on the corner of Main Street and Warren Street, high on a hill looking down on the town of Hayward. There were two large Bay Windows in the living room. One gave way to a view of Main Street, and the other viewed Warren. Directly across from the house on Main Street sat a Medical Complex, where all day long, people would park their cars in front of the house, get out, and pass right by the Bay Window, coming and going to one or another Doctor.

One of her favorite punishments to inflict on me was to summon me to the front Bay Window. There I am made to strip off my shirt and then stand at attention while she bound my hands behind my back with my belt. I sure got some strange looks from people who noticed me standing there as they headed towards the Medical Center and seeing me still standing there hours later upon their return. I spent many an afternoon in front of that Bay Window. Anytime I even thought about relaxing, she would put a strap across my back.

There was more punishment when my father came home. She would tell him whatever I had done to piss her off; of course, she never mentions the punishment she had already administered. Because of her, I would be summoned from my bedroom to be confronted by father; now, it was his turn to levy more punishment.

Usually, he made me take a large white kitchen dish towel and shape it into a diaper, and then I would strip naked so he could pin it on me. With that accomplished, the two of us would march down Main Street, heading towards the town. Father would let me have it across the back of my legs with the raiser strap he held in his hand like a whip, and all the while asking me if I had learned my lesson. Father paraded my diapered butt around town and through the Montgomery Ward Department Store at the corner of Main and A Street for any of my schoolmates who just might be in the store so they could get their jollies off, and then it was back up the hill to the house.

When we returned home, I am sent to my room, where I was to remain until the following day, when the daily ritual started all over again. The next day, the other kids who saw me in the diaper would tell the others, which caused me to get bullied.

Every time I did something that Alma did not like, there I was, standing in front of that Bay Window, and then came the diaper patrol. These abuse rituals continued from the middle of my sixth year of school and right up through the eighth year before I ever started fighting back by taking up the Martial Arts.

I woke up one morning with the thought that I had finally come to an awareness that I was fed up with Alma's punishments and Father's follow up and started rebelling at every chance. My first rebellion came when they went out to a neighborhood bar, and I was getting punished for eating cookies, of all things.

Before leaving the house, Father gave me instructions to sit on the living room sofa and watch the television while they were gone. Then he added, do not think of getting off that sofa, not even to change the television channel.

The event that led up to why I was, told to stay on the sofa all started one afternoon when Andrea, a female friend of Alma's, stopped by with a box of Danish cookies that she had baked and thought I might enjoy a few; the box held seven of them.

When I arrived home from school, I found Alma and Father not at home; however, Alma had left this note notifying me of the Cookies and Andrea's kindness. 'I did her gardening and cut her lawn each week for spending money.' The message stated Alma had put them in the cupboard for me.

Well, being thrilled about Andrea's thoughtfulness, I retrieved the Cookies and, with a glass of milk, in short order, I had eaten all of them; later that evening, father called telling me they would not be home for a few hours, and I should go to bed at my regular 6:30 P. M time. I hung up the phone, and when that time arrived, I went to bed.

When they arrived home as Alma passed by the trashcan, she noticed the empty box of Cookies and her message. For no other reason than being a bitch; she removed the evidence from the wastebasket, and what she did with it was anybody's guess but hers; however, then she came straight into my bedroom.

Of course, I was asleep and then woken by the feeling of something pulling at my hair, and the next thing I knew, the pulling got much more intense, and soon I am sitting on the bedroom floor; this was when I hear Alma saying.

"Listen to me, you little Son of a Bitching fagot, don't lie to me. Did you steal those Cookies Andrea brought by that I had put in the cupboard?"

Out of her yelling, what I heard I was something about having stolen the Cookies? Her question was a straightforward decision; Of course, I had not done such a thing because she had left me a note regarding the Cookies. Besides, how does one steal, what he has already been, given? So I answered her,

"No, I did not steal any Cookies. You're the one who left me a note telling me Andrea had brought them for me."

Alma replies.

"Don't be silly, you Asshole; I never left you any note."

With using a shoe for a missile, she went off on a bashing binge to my head while yelling.

"You are a damn liar, and how I know, I never wrote one. You are just making up shit, hoping your father will believe you and making me out to be some liar. Well, I got news for you; your father knows what a fricking liar you are, so you might as well confess you had to have stolen those Cookies."

Now father using his fist gets in on the bashing and before long my nose and mouth were squirting blood; I felt I had better start defending myself before I bled to death, and I yelled out.

"Father, she is lying. She left a note. If you do not believe it, then look in the garbage can. I did not steal those cookies. I ate them because her note said I could."

I hoped that after he found the note that his beating would stop, and he would see Alma was lying and not I; however, that is not to be the case. Father brought the garbage can into the bedroom and started going through it, looking for the note. When he could not find it, he smashes the trash box across my face and says at the top of his voice.

"You are a lying, Mother Fricker!"

He continued shouting every vulgar word he knew, and then he got a dictionary to find even more while continuing his rampage on my face. With one of his blows, it causes me to go flying onto the floor again, which gives into the moment needed for my father to realize his actions. With that calm came instructions on the way I was going to live out my upcoming punishment. I could not leave my room for three days, except to go to the bathroom, and no food or water.

You can bet something transpired in me that night, where I went from a scared young man to one any family member would be wise to fear. Should they choose to accuse me of something I had not done? When I had completed my punishment, Father and Alma made their pilgrimage to the Cazbar; their favorite bar, the following Friday night. Father tells me to sit on the sofa and watch the television; brother, that is just what I did. After five hours, I needed to relieve myself, but I wanted to obey like a good little dog, which meant not leaving that sofa. Therefore, I defecated while sitting there, and in doing so, it stains the couch.

When they returned home and found what I had done, they were furious; however, I was laughing in their faces. Father grabbed me by the throat and shoved me to the floor while again calling me several unknown names. While I am still on the floor, Father tor-off my pajamas and then rubbed the contents in them all over my face; then he grabs my left ear and starts pulling me to the shower. After I had washed, I was back in my room, which became my prison cell by now. The next day, Alma had to put makeup on my face to go to school; however, I was still laughing.

After what Alma pulled, I knew I needed to get as far away from her and Father. However, being an underage operator, where is it I thought I could go? The only place that came to mind was going back to living with mother. Reluctantly, I wrote, begging her to let me live with her again. My only dilemma is which one is the worst, Alma or Cal.

Mother writes back and says she had discussed the thought of me coming to Northlake with Cal; he agreed after she threatens to leave him if he had any problem with me coming there to live. I knew the only reason she had gotten him to agree; she had plans to cheat and needed a babysitter. When I approached father about the idea, he said.

"I am so glad to get rid of you because you are just a fricking fagot troublemaker."

That sounded as if he was more than happy to put me on an airplane heading for O'Hara International Airport.

When I arrived in Northlake, Illinois, Mother, Cal, and Melvin were living in the upper part of my Aunt Mary and Uncle Bill's home; two relatives I dearly loved; they both treated me like one of their own.

I had not been living there long before mother gave birth to another step-brother, whom she named Ricky. On that very afternoon, after bringing him home from the hospital, she returns to her old tricks.

Cal is working the night shift, so Mother waited for him to leave, and then she leaves Ricky and Melvin in my care while she headed out of the house looking for a party. When Cal returned home and found her gone, he became furious and went out to find her. Four days later, after beating her half to death, they returned.

With mother back home, she and Cal continually fight day after day. One late afternoon, as I was just about to climb the stairs leading to the upstairs, I could hear Mother and Cal arguing. As I am standing at the bottom of the stairs looking up towards the top suddenly, Mother, being naked, starts coming down the stairs screaming.

I was used to seeing her butt naked from Cal; always tarring her close off was not something I had never seen before. She continued down the stairs and ran into the kitchen where her brother Bill is sitting at the kitchen table. When he sees her naked and how badly beaten she was, his temper flared. And of all people to come walking into that kitchen is Cal; seeing him, Uncle Bill jumps from the table, and the fight is on.

Between the two, everything in the kitchen became airborne before Bill had beaten Cal half to death. There is nothing funny about that fight; however, before it started, Aunt Mary had been cooking a pot filled with Cow's Tongue. When the match ended, that tongue is hanging out of a hole in the wall, and how it got there is Cal had grabbed the pot off the stove and tossed the container at Uncle Bill, and when he ducks, it embedded itself in the wall.

After their fight, Uncle Bill gave mother the choice of staying without Cal or take Cal and her family out of his house. Mother remains with Cal, and within a day, every one of us is loading the car, and shortly after that, we were down the road headed for California.

The little ones were safely stowed in the third seat of Cal's 1954, Ford Station Wagon, and Mother and Cal were sitting in the middle chair drinking their whiskey and chasing it with beer. Of all people, I am the one elected to drive, even though I am underage to own a driver's license. I was to take the first four-hour shifts. However, it turned into four days; I drove the entire way without ever seeing the first police officer.

With us all now returned to Niles, it made me ecstatic to think I would soon see Poncho again, and being able to live with my grandparents is a plus. While in Illinois, my grandparents moved from their apartment above the Theater to a four-bedroom home on Second Street. Next to their house, several feet from the back of it, they built a large manufacturing facility, and they were producing salad dressing under the label, Grandmother Lee's Exclusive. Mother became a sales representative, and Cal had found work in the highway construction field.

Mother was never happy selling salad dressing, so she would hang out at the local San Francisco bars, meeting men that could give her a climax for the day. However, somehow she got a big contract with the Safeway food store chain; it would be her last.

Each morning in Niles, she would load her car with sample cases of the dressing and leave for the day, supposedly to find new Clients. Of course, as we know, that is not what she does; instead, she tosses the samples into the San Francisco Bay on her quest to find the nearest bar.

She continued getting away with it every day until someone had seen all the bottles piled up along the shoreline of the Bay inlet and brought it to the attention of City officials. Understanding the company addresses on the bottles, grandfather is contacted, and that is the last time Mother ever sold 'Grandmother' Lee's Exclusive Salad Dressing."

Chapter 4: You Both Rest in Peace

Each day after school, Poncho and I would set out to the factory and load trucks heading to Safeway Stores. One of my fond remembrances as a youth is when grandmother Poncho and I would have late summer afternoon talks after the salad dressing machines stopped for the day. One of those days, she told us about what the Guardian Angels were,

Grandmother, "I don't know if you boys know what a guardian angel is; it's a spirit that watches over you."

Grandmother dearly loved me and truly believed I had an extraordinary Guardian Angel.

Grandmother, "Understand, a Guardian Angel is someone who protects you. Some people call it your conscience; it is that gut hunch we have about everything we do. When you are deciding, your Guardian Angel lets you know which direction to take. However, you must listen to that voice in your head, or maybe, that strange feeling pulling at your gut."

We boys were not too sure what she was saying; however, out of that conversation, we got the message to listen to our intuition. I did not have the heart to tell her; if what has happened to me so far in my life is because of a Guardian Angel, I was not sure if I wanted one.

I grew another two years living in Niles, and that meant I was a lot, "Street Punk Wiser." I had become more independent and not having anything to do with any of my family members except my grandparents, my step sister Eva, and my two step-brothers, and Poncho.

I would not attend school unless I could walk there, no school bus for me. Of course, why not refuse the ride when Poncho and I would rather walk the three miles from town, especially with the excitement of the challenge of crossing the half-mile train bridge, with nowhere to walk; except between the rails. Should a Train had come along, the only way off that bridge is to jump, and you were in the Alameda River someone hundred and seventy feet below.

At the other end of the bridge was a railroad switch tower with a lone operator sitting. The building sat at a crossroads where the north, south, east, and westbound trains crossed. From that crossroads, we would continue our walk to where the railroad service access road is and follow it until reaching Vallejo Mills Elementary, where we always arrived at school for the last bell.

One day, we were walking across the bridge when we encountered another boy. Poncho and the other boy get into an argument over who had more right to be on that bridge. I took about as much as I was going to hear and walked over to the boy, grabbed him, and tossed him over the bridge railing, and he went free-falling into the water below, where he went straight under. Poncho, and I stood looking down, watching the boy trying to get out of the fast-running waters. I realized that day I was possible to kill someone, and never would I have a Conscience.

Each day, when school let out, we would once again head for the tracks. There, we would cross over and head down the hill on the other side to reach the Alameda River; that is where we would stop long enough to skip rocks or hit a fish trying to work its way upstream. We would continue downstream until coming to the only shallow point; there, we would cross to reach a hobo camp and listen in on all the many stories; from the countless places those hobos had traveled. When we got enough of that, we headed farther down the trail and stopped at the restaurant, where grandmother always had a piece of warm apple pie, with the coldest ice cream dumped on top.

Life was not too shabby, considering I had managed it around Mother and Cal. However, the day came where gut must have been sleeping or thought I did not have enough sadness in my life.

It happened the night when Poncho and I were tired of running the streets, jumping fences, and collecting bottles, we headed over to Poncho's house. His mother was a deaf-mute, and his father had died of cancer a month after Poncho's birth, so to make money to support her household, she took in laundry, cleaned houses, and did some cooking for a few people.

Upon entering the house, we heard what sounded as if someone is breaking up the entire place. The sound is coming from the rear of the house in Poncho's mother's bedroom. Poncho took off running towards the bedroom. And there, he finds two of four men raping her and beating on her at the same time. The other two men were going through her dresser drawers. What they were looking for only they knew. What were for sure two of those men were the same ones who killed Angus.

Understandably, Poncho's instinct to protect his mother came forth; he ran to the kitchen and grabbed a knife. Upon returning to the bedroom, he makes a dive on the bed and grabs a handful of the man's hair, holding his mother down; then slits his throat; he then grabbed the other man penetrating her, and slits his as well. The other two men jump Poncho, and while he is down on the floor, one man held him there, while the other man kept kicking him until rendering him unconscious.

I jumped on top of the man holding Poncho; however, he tossed me over into a corner of the room. When I got to my feet, I am stunned, yet not amazed enough not to notice the two men coming towards me. Glancing over at Poncho, I could see he is dead; they had already slit his throat several times, and when I looked back to the two men, they were now coming for me; I knew I had to get out of there or end up like Poncho and his mother.

I ran as fast as my legs would carry me out the front door, and I kept running until I realized they had stopped chasing me. I am now out of breath, too scared and concerned about what had just happened. As my breathing slowed, my curiosity came to the front burner of my thoughts, and I headed back to the house.

When I got there, I made it as far as the front porch, where I noticed at my feet. There is the butcher knife one man had thrown at me. I picked it up, turned, and went back into the yard, where I hid in the bushes out in front. From my visual point, I could see the two men and remained in hiding, waiting for them to come out of the house. Like a flash, I went out of the bushes when they do, and they came straight for me. The first man who came at me swinging his knife soon found his throat slit, while the other man soon noticed his guts were falling out of his body and splattering to the ground.

With what had just happened and dead bodies everywhere, I had found the courage to proceed back into the house. I took a moment to look up the street to see if the road is clear or if any neighbors had come out. However, the night is calm, with only the scent of death in the air.

I strolled up to the porch, entered the house, and headed for the back bedroom. The room, the floor, walls, and the ceiling is, spattered in blood. Poncho lies on the floor, and his mother is on the bed; her penetrators had not just stabbed her to death. They slit her vagina to her chest and then slit open both her breast. As for Poncho, they had slit his throat several more times, cut off his penis, and shoved it down his mother's throat.

I left the house in shock, and by the time I left the area, dismembered body parts were all around the yard. Who cut them up? That is the talk for years hanging over the town and a question that I will never divulge its answer.

Early the following day, when the carnage is, discovered when a neighbor noticed wild dogs were feeding off what looked like the head of one man. The event had such a profound effect that I went from some street punk to being possessed by the Martial Arts.

When grandfather came to his restaurant the following day, his earliest customers came in, telling of the horrible crime that had taken place over on Third Street. Shortly after that, I walked in, and grandfather came up to me with curiosity written on his face, wondering if I had heard what had happened; my cold and collected answer was.

"Yes, I not only heard, but I was also there."

There is no emotion on my face, and though grandfather's curiosity wanted details, something about that look on my face said silence might be the only answer he is going to get. I had emotions all right combined with feelings, the kind that has stayed within the confines of my already demented thoughts, along with much other than life's sad memories.

Without Poncho, I kicked rocks around Niles for a few more months as a loner. In time, my life got somewhat back to normal if there is such an entity. However, my days with Niles were about to end. Cal had taken a job at the Town House Nightclub in the town of Seaside, California. However, that move was short-lived because mother moved the family farther down the coast in the City of Pacific Grove, where they rented an entire boarding house and started renting the rooms as bed-and-breakfast.

I could have a dog; I got a Samoan Husky that came with the name, Samantha; that I shorten to 'Sam.' If we were not out of the Pebble Beach Golf Course along the Seventeen Mile Drive, we were on Oceanside at Lovers Point Park in Pacific Grove, or over in Monterey, the town next door hanging out on the Pier.

Whoever said, a dog being man's best friend is right on. In a precise short time, I had felt a secure friend connection to Sam, like no other in my past; every day, I would teach her new tricks. The dog was so superior that I signed her up for an upcoming dog show.

It was on a Friday, one day before the show. All I could think of is getting home from school and putting Sam through all her tricks to prepare for the show. As I approached the house, Sam is not there with her usual greeting. I looked around the yard before going into the house, thinking she somehow cannot get out the door. When I entered the house, there is no dog to be found there either. I asked mother if she had seen Sam, and she said.

"I don't have the time to look after some aged dog."

Cal walked in, and I asked him if he had seen Sam, and he said,

"I had the damn dog put to sleep! You got a problem with that you can set off back to you re father."

"Cal, why would you do such a thing?"

Cal, "I am tired of feeding an animal that likes you and your mother more than it likes my boys and me. If you don't like that, then you can get the hell out."

"Your day will come, Cal. You can count on it!"

After that conversation, Cal called my father and told him I had threatened to kill him and told him he did not want me living in his house. Before I knew it, Father and Alma were pulling up in front of the house.

When I lived in Pacific Grove, Eva had gotten married to a man named Jimmy and moved to Irvington, California. Uncle Ira had talked his parents into going into the dairy business with him on his Victor Montana farm. They sold their restaurant, gasoline station, home, and salad dressing business, and left Niles forever.

The ride back to father's house had made me feel as if I was going to my funeral. I might as well have been dead; at least I felt that way; I knew one detail for sure. There would be no Alma terrorizing me.

When we finally arrived at the house, I no sooner entered the door than I felt as if life had just sucked out of me. Everywhere I looked; there is a reminder of the abuse, beatings, punishments, and several more unfortunate events that had already taken place between Father, Alma, and me.

As I stood there in the living room, receiving my new orders, there is no doubt Alma was still the Sergeant. I had one factor going for me for the past years; true to my word, I had been continually training in the Martial Arts, and that gave me a bit of an edge should Father or Alma beat on me. Then also, I was much older now and more hardened.

There will not be any more morning inspections, no exams, and definitely, anyone trying to stand me up in front of a Bay Window would surely meet a premature death. However, that never stopped Alma's continually letting me know whose house I lived in daily. I still had house chores to do up to, and sometimes past the time, I would usually leave for school. Just like years earlier, I ran all the way to get there before the last bell; four tardiness days amounted to one cut day, and the school made sure it is on a person's report card.

Some things may have changed; however, her verbal abuse continued day after day, and from time to time, I would plead with father.

"I don't know how much more abuse I can take from Alma. Can't you please talk to her?"

He is quick to remind me she is his wife, and I must respect her as if she is my mother. You can bet how I answered that statement!

My life, when father is not around, remained in hell. Ironically, for whatever reason, I finally listened to my gut feelings, the actual gut feelings that grandmother had once mentioned.

For Father, Alma, and me getting along, it seemed impossibility no matter how I tried to be the model teenager, like; when the day came when it is my birthday, father let me go to the movies, which is a total surprise. However, it is better than spending the day locked in my room.

I had gotten up early, dressed, and slipped into the bathroom to wash up and then left the house. Being it is Saturday; I knew Father and Alma would spend their day at the Shamrock Bar on east 14th Street, right across the street from the Theater. The path I took that morning is to walk up to the top of Warren Street that dead-ended into M Street. Standing up that high on the hill, I could look out over Hayward. M. Street ran along the side of the cliff, running from the top of Warren Street to the bottom of Hotel Street. On one side of M Street, there is a grassy hillside, and on the other is a cliff that dropped straight off. If anyone were to look over the edge, what he or she would see is a Nash Automobile Dealership below. The Dealership would back their new-parked cars up against the wall of that Cliff.

I continued walking down M. Street, and turned right on Hotel Avenue, and kept walking until I reached east 14th Street; from there, right across the street to the Ritz Theater. The movie of the day is South Pacific, and with nothing else better to do, when it ended, I would watch it repeatedly until it is time to return home. I never knew people could be as happy as they were in that movie.

I crossed east 14th Street, headed up Hotel Avenue, and then started the climb on M. Street. During that walk, I passed by several boys higher on the grass hillside who were throwing rocks down on those brand new cars parked at Cliff's edge. Being older and more prominent, I stopped them and ran them off, and continued my climb.

Monday afternoon, when I returned home from school, there is a police officer in the house talking to Father and Alma. Seeing me, the police officer says.

"I'm looking around the neighborhood for who's seen someone throwing rocks on automobiles parked below the Cliff over on M. Street."

Before I could give my answer, father Spoke up and said to me,

"Boy, you came up M street Saturday. Did you see anybody?"

As far as I was concerned, I had run the boys off and could not see why I should involve them or me. If they were to be found, then let the police find them. So I answered.

"No."

Father would not let it go away and returned.

"Boy, you must have had something to do with it because you had come up M. Street on Saturday."

I replied, "What do I walking up a street last Saturday? Make you think I had something to do with rock-throwing?"

Before Father could give his answer, Alma sided in, making the same statement as father had. Finally, I hear from my gut.

"Confess to doing it, and father can pay for the damages."

I looked right at the police officer and said, "Ok, it was me who was throwing rocks down on those automobiles."

Alma said, "I told you. Your fagot son is nothing but trouble, the lying Son of A Bitch."

That confession cost me two weeks in the Alameda County Juvenile Detention Center. However, that did not bother me, exchanging one prison cell for another, thanks to my family; I had been spending many years already locked up in my bedrooms, their chosen prisons for me. Therefore, the Detention Center was only going to be a different jail cell, but with a lock on the door. At least I would be fed three times a day. Therefore, any jail cell was excellent, as long as it was away from Father, and Alma, who I considered idiots.

While in detention, a strange phenomenon took place. Each day, Alma would take a bus from Hayward and came to visit. It is the first time I had known of her being kind; of course, I felt she might protect her Ass by her kind deed. The last issue she wanted is her treatment towards me to come out in court, and my father finding out that her abuse was actually real. She, of all people, realized how much of a deep hatred I had for her, and now, she wanted to bury the Hatchet sort-to-say.

During my hearing, Alma told the court what an elegant teenager I was and that this incident with the automobiles is just a teenager blowing off steam. She also mentioned that father had already made full restitution to eight thousand dollars; I get placed on probation.

After returning home, the first matter on my mind is to find those five boys who had thrown the rocks and bringing them to confront father so that I could laugh in his face. I did not need to look far to find them. They were back on the hillside, tossing rocks. I tried asking them nicely to come with me and explain to my father that it is they who damaged those cars; however, they combated by throwing rocks at me, and that left me no other choice than to beat each one half to death; It was funny how that got their attention?

When they confess their crime to Father and Alma, they noticed how beaten up the boys were. After telling their stories, Father and Alma realized their stupidity caused me to say such a lie, which caused father; to be obliged to pay for damages that otherwise would have been the responsibility of those boys and their parents. Now that Hatchet, the one Alma wanted to bury, is aimed right at my head, and never again would there be a chance for Father, Alma or me, to mend our differences. Down the road, father never understood the reason to why the fathers of those boys who had thrown the rocks repaid him for all the damage their boys had caused. It was the least I could do.

Life continues; I am in my senior year of high school, and the work Alma piled on me each morning still caused me to run the rest of the remaining school year just to get there on time. When the School year ended, despite her, I graduated with straight A's. That day as I was walking home, being such a proud fellow, I had forgotten about Alma being the devil who was waiting at home. When I arrived, the first obsession I had is to show her my report card. Of course, her being this natural bitch, only concentrated on the four cuts on the report card and started yelling, and I replied.

"You have plenty of nerve, you bitch. Yes, Alma, that is what I said, you bitch. This crap is over; I am no longer taking anything from you, and I imagine I will tell everyone just what you have been doing to me all these years. O' and those School cuts are your fault, so get over It,"

Alma, "You wait till your father comes home, and if you say anything about me, he won't believe you because he thinks you're a fagot."

By the time father arrived home from work, I had cut the front yard with my report card folded in my shirt pocket. I ran to him to show him the report card. He looked at it and acted proud, and congratulated me, and then headed into the house with the report card in his hand. I returned to cutting the lawn, and when finished, I came into the house where I overhear Father and Alma discussing the cuts on the report card. When father noticed me standing behind him, he turned and questioned me about why I had been cutting classes? I started explaining when Alma jumped into the conversation.

"The Son of a Bitch has been skipping school."

Hearing this, I yelled out.

"You're a lying bitch. You're just afraid I might tell father how you have been treating me all these years?"

Now I did it! Father throws the report card down and, with his fist; hits me across the side of my head, and then grabbed me, and throws me through the kitchen door; the one is leading to a connecting garage, and I land on the cement floor with father, right after me, kicking me in the teeth.

Enough was enough; I snap, and like some rocket lifting off, I jumped to my feet like some Ninja Warrior, and on one leg, I spun around and put my shoe to his face. With that kick, his face was pouring out blood as he lay on the garage floor. I knew when he came two, and I would be sent to my bedroom. Therefore, I just took it upon myself to head there.

An hour later, Father and Alma are outside on the patio. I was still in my room and sitting on the bed when I felt my gut tugging, letting me know it is time for me to move on. I was finished with school, nineteen years old, and I knew when father confronted me, he would kick me out. I mentally spoke to my gut.

"Ok, where will we head off to?"

The message that returned is.

"Not to worry, I will guide you."

Without another thought, I chose my cowboy boots to wear, a lightweight jacket, and then opened a box that I kept under my bed and took out what money was in it from mowing grass. I walked to the bedroom door, opened it slowly, stuck my face out, and looked around for Father and Alma. I could hear them talking out on the back patio, and my gut let me know it's do or die time, and quietly I took myself out of the front door. Once outside, I ran and ran until I was out of breath; then I realized I was running for new freedom. No longer was I going to put up with the likes of Father and Alma. I felt what the slaves must have felt getting their freedom after years of punishment.

With the money I had in my box, I headed to the Greyhound Bus Station, and I bought a ticket as far as the money would take me, and that was Cheyenne, Wyoming. From there, I planned to hitchhike on to Franklin Park, Illinois, where my Aunt and Uncle lived. I arrived in Cheyenne late in the afternoon and headed for the outskirts of the town. I got a bit of luck when the first car that came along pulled up. Within a few miles down the road, the man and I had gotten acquainted enough for the man to ask me if I would mind if we pulled over in the next town at Kimball, Nebraska, so he could get some badly needed sleep before continuing. I felt the man be sincere and told him I saw nothing wrong with his request.

No sooner had the man turned into a Cemetery and turned off the ignition, did he reach over, grab me by my throat, and ordered me to let him suck my penis, words I had heard elsewhere in life? While the man is trying to get my penis out of my pants, I heard from my gut.

"At your feet is a tire-changing iron. Grab it, and use it."

Using my foot to search for the tire iron, when I felt the tool, I immediately pulled away from the man, reached down to the floorboard, picked it up, and beat it into the man's face. With every swing out of me came all the hate and punishment I had already accumulated throughout my life. Within seconds, the man was a bloody mess, and blood is everywhere.

The man was slumped over his steering wheel as I was hurriedly jumping out of the car; still holding on to the tool; I went around to the driver's door to see if the man is dead. I felt him still breathing. Before I had opened the car door, I had decided that if the man is alive, I will make sure he died for what he wanted to do to me.

Knowing the man is alive, I started beating him again with the tool until he stopped moving. It is now that I realized I had better leave the area and getting free from my sexual predator. However, I stopped in my tracts and looked back towards the car, wondering if I had succeeded in actually killing the bastard or just knocked him unconscious.

I returned to the car and ripped the man out on the pavement, and then took the tool and continued beating him some more. However, I was just getting started. More blood now is gushing from the man when I jump in his car, started it, and ran over the man as countless times as I felt justified. When I walked off this time, the man is pinned under the left front wheel with the tire itself smashing down on his neck, and the other side of the tire is doing the same to his face. Then a thought came to me.

"If one should have to die, where better to be than a Cemetery?"

I crossed the Lincoln highway only when there were no oncoming cars. Once on the other side, I started walking. Every time another vehicle is about to pass, I am ducking among the tall grasses and reeds along the roadside.

About an hour into my plight, night has fallen. I came upon a farmhouse, and lucky for me, garments were hanging on the clothesline. Another bit of luck came when I noticed there must have been a teenager living there my size, and I took what clothes I needed since I was covered in drying blood.

I continued my westerly journey from that farmhouse, making sure I remained in the fields instead of the road's shoulder. Through the night, I kept walking until coming upon a horse, troth. There, I wiped the tire iron and tossed it out into a pasture, then stripped and jumped into the cold water to wash off. Now that I was redressed, I continued walking back towards Cheyenne.

Coming upon a large tree, I rested until daylight. As I am leaning against a tree through the night air, I can hear a siren far off coming from the direction over by the highway. When it stopped, I wondered if it might have been at the Kimball Cemetery. I waited an hour before I once again hear the siren through the dark of night. I'm hoping it was an ambulance speeding to some hospital or more like the morgue, if I am lucky.

When quietness returned to the night, I fell asleep. The morning dew wakes me. And now I consider my chances of going out on the Lincoln, hoping to catch a ride through to Cheyenne and on westward. Again, my gut gave me the answer. It is my lucky morning because the first car of the day stopped, and its occupants were going straight through to Rawlins.

Reaching Rawlins, I am once again hanging out with my thumb. Unfortunately, because I did not listen to my gut this time, my afternoon is not as lucky as the morning was. I was standing curbside, right in downtown Rawlins, when a police car pulled up and arrested me for breaking the Rawlins law; no hitchhiking within the City Limits ordnance. My gut was letting me know I should I walk the ten-block hamlet until I reached the City Limits sign before sticking out my thumb.

I remain in jail for seven weeks, and the only way I was going to be released is to contact someone back in Hayward to send me the money it is going to take for a bus ticket out of Rawlins. Through a friend Roger, he sends me a bus ticket; a police officer put me on a westbound bus.

Chapter 5: From Teenager to Adulthood

When I arrived in Hayward, Roger offered me a place to stay with him and his Mother. I remained with them most of that summer, working construction for Roger's uncle driving a dump truck. He and I were on the cleanup crew and would remove the debris at every home built in a housing development. While working, an Italian family had purchased a track home, and their daughter and I hit it off, which led to us having sex. She was my first. Afterwards, I felt as if I had committed the biggest crime in history. No one had ever explained sex to me; all I ever heard was never to touch a girl, and if I did, I would commit some sin. I was scared to death of what might happen to me if anyone found out what we did; what if she tells someone? All I could think of; I was going to be, locked up for the rest of my life, and that thought gives way to giving me a reason to leave Hayward forever.

Desperate time needs desperate measures, and I would not be picky about where I went; it had to be far away. Where to go is my only dilemma because my single worldly travels being on my own so far had only taken me to some Cemetery in Kimball, Nebraska. Then my gut suggested,

"Why not go to Salinas because you still have to settle up with Cal for what he had done to Sam."

Therefore, with the gained knowledge that Cal and Mother were living in Salinas, that is where I headed. Through my Uncle Howard, I got mother's phone number and called and explained I wanted to move out of Hayward, and I was no longer living with father. She told me they had plenty of room; within a week, I am boarding a Greyhound Bus.

To my surprise, at the Salinas terminal, instead of mother waiting, Cal is there waiting with a friend named Kenny. Stepping off that bus was the turning point in my life. It's not just coming to Salinas; somewhere between Kimball, Nebraska and Hayward and then coming to Salinas, I began feeling as if I had gone through some transformation that started with my suffrage years as a youth and growing into a teenager and now into adulthood.

The roads I already traveled had taken me through some harsh tones, with the likes of a father, who loved my mother more than life itself. To Alma, Cal, and the likes of mother, who never, in fact, showed she was interested in children; however, she went on in life to have four. The tragic irony, Melvin and Ricky were now following the same roads as Eva and I had, somewhat unloved and unwanted.

Mother is approaching her senior years now, and as for her being the lovely good-time girl, that is withering away. For me, it is insignificant how she is aging. What is, is the years I felt of a lack of motherly love and discipline

What helped me get this far with life decisions is that I have a true free spirit. Feelings I once had about most things I disliked about my family were diminishing. That feeling gave me my perspective on life. Most of the awful feelings I had been carrying for years about Cal, Mother, Alma, and Father were also going by the wayside; however, Cal was not off my hook.

On the drive to the house, Kenny did most of the talking. And my gut is letting me know we would become the best of friends, despite him being forty years my senior. He worked for one of the junior high schools in Salinas as a groundskeeper. However, he had an enjoyable hobby; for the better part of his life, he had been a Mechanic, i.e., 'a mafia Hit-Man' the Mechanic no one ever expects, because of his warm, helpful, and kind demeanor. At one time in his life, he had played in Cal's band in the early Niles years.

Once I got settled into my new scene, Kenny and I started spending many hours together with him explaining the unpleasant facts of life, and I even got some insight into why mother lived the life she has. It got so that I spent a great deal more time at Kenny's home in Castroville than I did with Cal and Mother in Salinas.

I had learned to drive a car through a friend of father's years earlier, and through my friend Roger, I had gotten my CDL license. However, I had yet to renew my driver's license, and Kenny loaned me his 1955 Cadillac for the test. After that, Kenny loaned me another car of his a 1954 Mercury that was gathering dust sitting out in his driveway. By using the Mercury, I learned the town of Salinas, and in doing so, I learned about dragging the Main.

Before long, Kenny suggests he is taking me as his apprentice to learn the art of being a Mechanic. He said what made me a superior candidate; he could see I have minimal sympathy for humankind. Over the coming years, though, Kenny, I've become an expert on human elimination!

With my good looks, I had no problem filling up the Mercury with girls who wanted, too, dragging the Main. Each night, I would be parked on some side street, making out. It is while dragging the Main where I met Marion. She lived across the road alongside the Salinas High School, and I lived across Main on Willow Street with Cal and Mother. We dated for a few months until the night we were making out in the back seat of my car. When things got heated, I put my hand between her legs; however, this horrible smell came with it when I pulled my hand out. It is so bad that I made her get out of the car. I never saw her again. I had smelled nothing like it since; it left me with another reason to wonder about girls.

A party took place at Cal and Mother's house, and I ignored my gut again, warning me not to attend. During the evening with Cal, being intoxicated, he became determined to prove to mother who is the better man, he, or me. Of course, what Cal is not aware of about my reasoning for coming to Salinas in the first place was he? It is to get revenge, and therefore, there would not be a moment where I am letting my guard down, and for sure, I will not take one bit of abuse from the man and with him not having any common sense, I am on my guard throughout the evening.

I am standing in the kitchen when, without warning, Cal took his fist and smacked me across the side of the head. The backlash caused the insanity in me to emerge, and instantly, that puts Cal on the floor, gasping for breath. Unfortunately for him, I continued delivering deathblow after deathblow. If it were not for mother pleading for me to stop, I would have killed him. Beating him started a more profound craving, and that meant there would never again come a moment where my stepfather would have the chance to hit me. Of course, I still am not through with Sam's revenge as long as Cal is alive. When I stopped beating him, he is upside down in an outside garbage receptacle.

It took another year for Cal and me to have our second go-around to come about. Mother had invited me on a camping trip over by Hollister at the Pinnacles Campgrounds out on the Airline Highway on Road 146. We had arrived mid afternoon on a Friday, and during that afternoon, I learned from other campers that there would be a dance-taking place at the Campground Pavilion. As soon as the evening meal is over, I headed over there. I'm standing alongside the dance floor talking with two girls when Cal approached; he gets right up in my face and says,

"I'm going to prove once and for all to your mother, you bastard, that I am the better man."

I looked right into his eyes and said,

"I strongly suggest you turn around and head back to the campsite before you get more of me than you could ever imagine in your lifetime."

About then, I noticed Cal's fist coming towards me, and on instinct, I reacted and came close to ripping his jugular out of his body. Within seconds, with one kick, I had removed every tooth the man had. I drew out his left eye from its socket with one finger before sending a round of punches between his legs; I had become once again a killing machine.

He dropped to the ground with his head falling between two rock boulders that lined the parking area, and while he was stuck there, I jumped up and down on his head. Because I was determined to kill him, it took four big men to pull me off him.

Cal is left with several ribs broken, blood gushing everywhere, an eye dangling, brain concussion, plus a cracked skull. What is so uncanny is how I instantly, after almost killing the man, lost every bit of my anger I had for him and even helped him into the ambulance. Because of that fight, the camping trip is cut short. After returning home, I went to the hospital to see if Cal is still breathing; to my surprise, he tells me.

"Just wait until you become twenty-one, and then we will see who the best man is."

I started laughing and said.

"Seriously, dude, man, you've got balls, and you have a date. I only wish I were turning twenty-one right now. That beating was for Sam; however, you can be sure of one thing; since I didn't kill you this time, I will the next time around."

I could not wait for that day when I got that rematch.

I left the hospital and got on with my life. Before long, I had taken an interest in what is called Numerology, the art of learning a person's personality and social traits by assigning numbers to the letters of their name. I started learning what secrets might be behind the dominant art form like a madman to a significant extent, as I had with learning Martial Arts to being a Mechanic until I had mastered those subjects. It was the same with Numerology, at least enough to test its theory, which is if one changes one's name, it changes one's fate and one's personality.

I have lived through a couple more birthdays with no person trying to govern my life. I had made my own decisions, giving me some insight into what kind of man I will become in comparing it to my surroundings growing up. From here on, I could do things I never had done before or even had any interest in doing. Like, owning my first car, that put me each night after work of dragging up and down Main Street or parked at Mel's Drive-in until late at night.

For girls, I had gained many misgivings about them over the years. So not to be biased, I had the same thoughts about men. Having consensual dating was so much different from forced relationships on my body, and I now realize what other things there were in the world besides abuse.

One evening, while dragging the Main, I meet Rayna and how that happened. As I drive past the Theater, I noticed that sitting in the ticket booth is this blond. Of course, that blond hair alone in a well-lighted box would get any man's attention.

From that first time I saw her, and every night after, I would drive by with a beep of the horn, and she would wave. Finally, I got up enough nerve to park long enough to walk up to the ticket window and ask her name. From that day forward, she and I would drag the Main every night after her shift ended.

We were sitting in Mel's Diner one Friday evening eating a hamburger or two when a Blue 1959 Chevrolet Impala Convertible came pulling into the space alongside us. Behind the wheel is an olive skin, quite overweight person? Before long, he and I had started a conversation discussing cars; his name was Ronny Sutfin. From that night forward, we would run into one another out on the Main, and over time, we had befriended one another, nothing like it was with Poncho. However, it was the first time since his death that I even considered another male friend.

Ronny lived at the junction of Jolon and Mission roads in Jolon, California, in Monterey County. His mother had a contract with the Army to operate at that location, a Grocery Store, Restaurant, Service Station, Post Office, and Trailer Park. It was located some sixty-five miles south of Salinas at an elevation of 971 feet in the San Antonio River Valley. About 6 miles up the road is Mission San Antonio de Padua and Fort Hunter Liggett. The small communities, sat right in the middle of the Hunter Liggett Military Reservation.

Ronny, just like me, had been brought up in an abusive environment until he was adopted. However, since then, his adoptive father had passed because of old age, leaving his adoptive mother to take care of him, whom he loved to call 'Lubster'.

During the workweek, Ronny attended college in Salinas and camped out there at his sister's house. When he was not in school, he worked at the Shell Gasoline Station on South Main Street. Every Friday night after dragging the Main, he would travel home to help his mother over the weekend.

I had gotten a part-time job at the Hancock Service Station next door to the Shell Station. Each night, when Ronny and I got off work, we would get into his Chevrolet Convertible, with its top-down unveiling its bright red interior, and drag the Main. It was a nightly ritual, remaining as fresh as the rest of the street dragsters.

Cruising was an art form; it usually kicked off at Mel's Drive-in on the south end of town. Then it is a drive two blocks north to cruise through Fosters Freeze parking lot; that was necessary before heading back out on the Main. Still headed north, we would pass the service stations where we both worked. With them being closed for the night, the parking lots doubled as the showplace for all the

Custom Cars parking there, with their front ends facing the Main. Continuing north, passing the Salinas High School, then up a few blocks to the Theater where Rayna worked, then circle the block and retrace our route.

One night, Rayna introduced her best friend, Hope to Ronny, and from then on, there were four playing it cool on the Main. One night, when Rayna's parents went out-of-town, she and Hope invited Ronny and me over to Rayna's house to have intercourse. It only took Hope fifteen minutes before taking Ronny by the hand to lead him into Rayna's, mother's bedroom. Taking the second lead, Rayna took my hand, and we went into her father's bedroom where she had put down towels on the bed; she did not want any stains getting on the bedspread; right there, I got the impression she is not a virgin.

A few weeks later, I saw Rayna and drove right up upon her and her ex-boyfriend Robby making out in a car parked just down the street from her house. It caused us to break up. For me, life went on, as I had no misgivings about what a woman would or would not do or say.

Ronny and I got the crazy idea of renting a house together, one we could hold parties in, a twenty-four-hour party house, a place, far enough between any neighbors, so the noise would not bother them or the Police Department.

It did not take long to furnish it via help from our friends who also dragged the Main. Every weekend, the big parking lot surrounding the house remained jammed with cars.

By now, Rayna had faded into the sunset. And I am currently dating a girl named Frenchy. How I met her, I am at work pumping gas into a car when Davy G, another person I had befriended dragging the Main, pulls into the Station, stops right next to me and opens his passenger door, and pushes this girl out on the asphalt; she is naked. Davy G yelled at me.

"Hey, Rock! Her name is Frenchy, and she is all yours."

Of course, I knew Davy G, and she had been dating for months. I put my jacket around her and rush her into the service bay area of the Station. Lucky for me, it is right at closing time, and we headed for the party house.

For months, people continually kept coming and going. Even Rayna would come by. However, her new steady date is a soldier named David, stationed at the Fort Ord Military Base. Rayna had mentioned to me that when she met David, it is love at first sight, and she must have been telling the truth because, since her first time of bringing him to the parties, the two remained in a steamy romance Frenchy and I finally break up. Strangely enough,

David and I befriended one another; if there is a more unmatchable pair than us.

There is one night when I am on the Main driving Ronny's Convertible, with its own full-bore, three-forty-eight under the hood; I came upon David's exceptional Ford. I pulled alongside, and with one look over at one another, David nodded. And the race is on. Passing the Fosters Freeze, we both caught another gear, and by the time we passed the High School, both of us were traveling at full speed. Approaching the Theater, it is nose to nose as we caught another gear. I pulled-a-way and grabbed another gear when suddenly, the engine blows. There were engine parts all over the Main. David pulled away as the Convertible came to a dead smoking stop. He circled the block, then came back to help me tow the car back down the street to the Shell Station to be, repaired. Every night, David would drive over to Salinas from Fort Ord and show up over at the Shell Station to help Ronny and my rebuild.

When the car is running again, the three of us took it to Jolon. Going there is the bomb; because we had seven ice-cold coolers of beer to choose from and all the food, we could ever eat on the weekend. Of course, Ronny loved to hunt, and when his chores were, done, we would fully equip Ronny's Jeep with all the provisions needed to amass a full-scale war on the local Deer population, where the three of us would head off terrorizing the backcountry. When we were not drinking, hunting, or running motorcycles, all over the Reservation, we were seventeen miles back down the road in the town of King City, chasing girls.

Usually, if I am not at work or with David or Ronny, I could be, found with Candy, Dolly, and Quennie. I had met these three girls one late night at the North Main Street Pool Hall. Dolly had come up to me asking if I would give her and her two friends a ride home. When I got to their house, they insisted I come in. Once inside, the girls leave me in the front room, and there I wonder if I should go when one girl called out for me to come into the bedroom. I was not too sure if I should; however, curiosity got the best of me. I no sooner entered the room, where all three of them grabbed my body and pulled me onto the bed. The next thing I knew, I was coming up for air. They were bisexual and hooked over in Monterey. That night I took a "licking," if you get the meaning.

From that night forward, when I would drop by late at night, and we all piled up in bed and licked one another as if we were a bunch of lollipops. The girls were in the age range of five years or more my senior and those bisexuals taught me more at my age about female sex than most people would ever come to know in their lifetime. They had taught me all the anomalies and anthropology's on sex there is.

My thoughts of life were pretty darn good until trouble came the afternoon when David came to Linda's house, who, from time to time, she and I would have intercourse. Accompanying him is another soldier named Harry. The three of us headed to Monterey. David said we would need to cut through Fort Ord's east gate first because David wanted to pick up another soldier named Dwayne, who is on guard duty until midday; we arrive just as his shift ended. The four of us exited through the west gate onto highway 68 and continued our journey into Monterey, only stopping long enough to purchase a bottle of liquor from a bootlegger.

We had been at a beach on Sunset Drive, and the night is coming down as we continued passing the bottle and David suggested,

"Let's leave the beach and head over the hill to Carmel."

We took Sunset Drive to Congress Avenue, to Forest Lodge Road, to Congress Road, too, S F B Morse Drive. Halfway up, the S F B, Harry, and Dwayne started arguing over something that happened back at the Base a few days earlier. Their arguing gets so bad that David pulled the car to the side of the road. Harry, and Dwayne, took their grievances out onto the roadside, and as drunks will do, fist fighting breaks out, and it does not take long before Dwayne is flat on his face in the roadside gutter. About then, a car is coming, so David, Harry, and I head up on the hillside and hide in the brush and trees until it passed; as soon as it did, we came jumping off the embankment onto the road. Because it is so dark, none of us could tell where Dwayne is, and unfortunately, David and Harry landed right down on top of him. If Harry had not knocked him out, having two grown men jumping on your chest certainly should.

Harry tried to revive Dwayne with no success. While Harry is standing over Dwayne, another car is coming up the hill. David left Dwayne, and we jumped into the car and drove off. What David and I are not aware of, Harry had stolen Dwayne's wallet.

If that whole incident was not enough to get us in trouble, just a mile further up the hill is some girl hitchhiking. David makes a u-turn and heads back to where the girl is, and pulls up right alongside her. She is not too much for conversation; however, she said her name is

Becky and she is running away to anywhere she could get a ride. Harry spoke to her.

"Do you want a ride with us?"

Becky, "Where are you guys going?"

I spoke up and told her.

"We are going to visit my Uncle, who lives on the other side of King City." Then David jumps into the conversation.

"Yeah, girl, come with us, it is awful dark out here."

Becky, "How do I know you won't hurt me?"

About then, Harry had got impatient and jumped out of the car and lifts Becky off her feet, and put her in the backseat, and David drives off.

Wherever I had gotten the bright idea to head to Cal's brother Orland's house is anybody's guess. The man lived out on the Jolon road, within a mile of Ronny's place, someone hundred miles from where we were with Becky in the back seat. And since boys will be boys, sex became the moment, and our hitchhiker is more than willing to see that we get our needs met.

She said she is nineteen; however, none of us believed her or cared when she is undressing, and each one of us is concentrating on her naked body lying on the back seat. At least, I suggested to David and Harry that we should not have sex without her permission; however, that is a moot point when Becky said,

"I want to have sex."

Before driving off since David and Harry were already in the back seat, I took the wheel and would get my turn somewhere down the road. However, would you not know it; I drove to Orland's.

By the time we reached his house, the drunk we had been on is failing, and fatigue has set in, and we all crashed out on the living room floor. I was the first to wake, and the first thing I noticed was Becky is, gone, and I woke up the others with the news, and in a quick minute, the other two and we were doing a ground search to no avail. We returned to the house, and Orland had gotten up and had breakfast ready. Within an hour, we were, prepared to head back to Salinas. At the car, while we were saying our goodbyes to Orland, David yells out.

"Look, guys, on the road, that was Becky in the back seat of that passing Sheriff's car."

Sure enough, as the Sheriff's car passes by, sitting in the back seat is Becky. We figured she must have gotten up early and started her hitching, Harry said.

"Unfortunately, she didn't get far."

Chapter 6: Leaving Salinas

Two weeks later, I am in Traffic Court, answering why I shouldn't get charged for twenty-two traffic tickets I had run up over four months for drag racing down the Main. The Judge is not impressed with any thoughts I had and fines me for two hundred and twenty dollars. I had the pleasant news until five o'clock that very afternoon to pay those fines or spend twenty-two days in jail. As I am driving out of the City parking lot, I heard coming from my car radio.

"David Macklin, and Harry Cross, two Fort Ord soldiers were arrested today on charges of strong-arm robbery of another Fort Ord Soldier and lucid acts of sex with an underage girl; the third suspect is still at large."

Of course, this did not sit well, and the underage girl mentioned had to be that hitchhiker Becky; I was sure of it. However, the puzzling question is how did the Sherriff's department connect us to her? I do not think Becky knew whom Dave, Harry, and I am? Currently, I think a moot point considering the damage is, done. I am bright enough to know if I get picked up for what happened to the Soldier; even though I had nothing to do with her, I will get more time over Becky.

I needed to talk to David. That was, an impossibility, considering I could not show my face in the jail; a game plan was, needed.

I headed over to Cal and Mother's house because I had been long aware that Cal had befriended David, and he could get in the jail to talk to for me. Would he do that for me, or would I have to slam him up against a wall before he agreed to help me?

Cal fooled me when he said,

"Sure, I'll talk to him."

Cal agreed to go, and when he returned, I was waiting with mother.

Cal, "Well, I had a conversation with David, and he said the long arm of the law hasn't a clue about who is the other guy, and he and Harry aren't talking, so you're safe. He said the girl, this Becky couldn't identify you guys, or maybe she didn't want any remembrance of what everyone looked like?"

Me, "Man, I don't have a clue how the Sheriff's Office connected this Becky and us. That Soldier is a problem because he could identify me. Maybe I should leave town for a while."

Cal, "That might not be such a terrible idea because David said the Soldier is, being, shipped overseas soon. When he does, you could come back."

Me, "You're right; I am going to have a hard enough time raising enough money to pay for my ticket as it is, and I do not even have the money to leave. You got any cash I can borrow?"

Cal, "Don't look at me. We barely have enough ourselves to making it until payday. Why don't you sell your car? At least you can take a bus somewhere."

Me, "Well, maybe, however, I need to get the hell out of Salinas, and as fast as I can."

Leaving Salinas is a straightforward decision; however, where to go was the question. It would comprise somewhere where not anyone looking for me would ever figure I had gone. Then it came to me; Victor Montana. It is the perfect place, yet the ware how to get there is the task.

I got a bit of luck when I sold my car on such short notice. Unfortunately, that only got me enough money for a bus ticket as far as Reno, Nevada. From there, I would have to hitchhike the rest of my way. What would be the odds that, for the second time in my life, my money would only take me part of the way?

Between departing on that Greyhound bus and its pulling into the Reno terminal, it is as if I had entered another earth dimension. It is four in the morning, and my biggest concern is not having any money, which leaves me with the only obvious answer; come daylight, I will beat the streets looking for work.

It was early morning when I left the bus station coffee shop and headed out onto the streets. A motel a block away hired me to pull weeds for a dollar an hour with lunch included. With the eight dollars I earned, I paid seven of it for a room in the Biggest Little City in the World. I got up early the following day and checked out, and headed for the highway, hoping to catch a ride east.

From this moment on is where my life takes me on unbelievable adventures right into, for a better word, the "Twilight Zone."

None of my fresh adventures will ask me if I minded taking part, like my plight into Montana. That is so unforeseen. I will meet new and exciting people, further limitations, and the latest liabilities from here forward. Of course, my gut lets me know; hold on tight because I am heading for one hell of a roller coaster ride.

That roller-coaster ride started as I am standing out on the highway with my thumb out, and a Red 1940 Ford pickup stopped and picked me up. The driver, an eighty-four-year-old man according to him, said I am going as far as Salt Lake City, Utah, and as we traveled more now down the road, the more the older adult took a liking for me.

We arrived in Salt Lake City, which by now had already turned dark, and the older adult offers me a place for the night at his daughter- and son-in-law's home; the older adult is sure they would not mind, and he was right. I spent my first night in a Mormon home. Before that night, I had never heard of Mormon, and here they were offering me food and shelter. After the morning breakfast, the older adult made a phone call and got me a day's work in a warehouse; that gave me needed traveling money.

When the workday ended, I started walking towards highway 89, now heading north where once again, I am holding out the thumb. However, I never gave a thought about winter during that time of year, and it had just poked its ugly head out, causing the temperature to plummet into the low teens; however, luck is still on my side. I caught a ride with the first car coming down the road; the driver was a radio commentator from Twin Falls, Idaho, a place the man referred to as the "Magic Valley," i.e., a region in south-central Idaho comprising eight Counties. It is particularly associated with the agricultural sector in the Snake River Plain in that area.

At Twin Falls, I thanked the man, and once again, I am standing out in the cold on a dark highway. My luck was still holding, however, when I caught another ride with two brothers who are heading for Idaho Falls. It was past midnight by the time we arrived, and they let me out of their car at a truck stop. Outside, the air was chilling down into my soul; however, it is warm inside the truck stop restaurant.

With little money and certainly not enough for a rented room for the night, I had no choice except to continue north. After a couple of cups of coffee in an attempt at warming me, and thinking maybe someone might travel that late at night and might need company and pick me up.

I headed out into the cold and walked off up the ramp onto the highway above. I stood ankle-deep in snow as I kept folding my arms, bobbing up and down, trying to stay warm, while holding my hands over my face so what warmth I had left coming from my breath could keep my skin from freezing. Without a coat keeping the cold away, I wonder how I could even stand the temperature.

Out on that highway, it is so dark where I can barely see my surroundings, and it is as silent as if the earth had stopped its rotation, and the entire planet is void of life, causing a lonely feeling coming from within. If I am not cold enough, the snow falls harder.

The more snow falls, the colder I become until my stubborn self gives in, and I walk back down the ramp and back into the truck stop. As soon as I had gotten up more courage than I had the sense of taking part in, I returned to the frosty night. There I am, like some retard back dancing up and down in the deep snow when a car pulled up. The same two brothers that had dropped me off at the truck stop. They had gotten to wondering, with the horrible weather, if

I had gotten a ride. At least, I would not be cold the rest of that night because the brothers took me over to their house, where they offered me their couch.

Of course, after my Wyoming incident years earlier, the first thing coming to my mind are that these guys gay, or maybe, even serial killers; however, as cold as I am, I did not hesitate to get into their warm vehicle. The brothers were not gay or serial killers, just genuine people. Come morning, the three of us headed back over to the truck stop, and the brothers pay for breakfast then surprises me when they gave me some money before I made the trek back out on the snow-packed highway; what I needed more than money, is a warm coat.

As I am standing out here without a coat, the elements are a little more miserable. There is no ride in sight, yet the snow continues with light flurries, coming in dense patterns from time to time, whereby, late afternoon, I cannot feel my feet. With night falling and the weather has become even worse, just when I get to thinking of heading back to the truck stop, these same two brothers who gave me a ride to here are pulling up alongside. They are heading home and saw I still am out in the cold and suggest I spend the second night with them. The following morning, they've once again fed me, and when they leave the truck stop, they give me an elegant, warm, heavy coat.

That morning, the blizzard conditions had given way; however, cold and clear skies prevailed, and the first car coming along gave me a ride into Butte, Montana. The older adult, who picked me up, is a traveling salesperson that took the liking of his liquor more than his job. We would stop at every Tavern along the way. Before reaching Butte, the man is so drunk that I am doing the driving. At night, the salesperson paid for our rooms and dinner. In the morning, as soon as breakfast is over, we headed west towards Victor Montana. It is on Highway 12, at Garrison, where we parted. The salesperson was, headed for the town of Avon and then would head north towards Helmville.

Once again, there I am sticking out my thumb when a logging truck pulled up and took me as far as Missoula; from there, I had another thirty miles. I caught a couple of rides; however, I had to huff it into Victor. When I arrived at my grandparent's house, they were surprised to see me and greeted me with open arms. Within a few days, Uncle Ira is teaching me about milk cows, and every morning at five AM, I am in the barn. It is a beautiful farm, about a thousand acres, with 360-degree views of the Sapphire Mountains Ranges and breathtaking views of the entire

Bitterroot Valley. My grandparents live across the road from the main farmhouse in a small yet charming white Cottage surrounded by tall trees and a dirt ditch on three sides of the Cottage with water flowing into it.

When my work and chores around the farm were done, I would walk down the gravel road headed for the town of Victor and hang out at the only gas station with the other local teenagers living in the area. I remained in Victor through the end of winter before calling, mother and she tells me,

"The Soldier got shipped overseas, and David and Harry are in the brig at Fort Ord, over Harry's involvement with that Soldier. The girl, Becky, had identified no one."

Her information brought immense relief, knowing I am out of harm's way; of course, I still had the Salinas Court; however, I need not hide anymore.

With Montana's winter ending giving me a thought of leaving Victor; it is an excellent time to do it; I would to go to Sumner, Washington, where Rayna's older sister Jewel and her husband Cam live.

Grandmother expressed her wishes of having me remain on the farm. However, I had decided. Or a well-known entity called my gut told me it is time, a problem that presented itself. I have not a cent in my pocket, and the only money around is on the bedroom dresser in the coin book collection belonging to my Aunt and Uncle.

It was a frigid morning when I said my goodbyes to everyone and started my journey down the road towards the main highway. Passing the local gas station, I dropped in to say goodbye to my new friends that I knew I would never see again. I continued my walk out to the main highway, and there I started thumbing, hoping to catch a ride into Missoula.

I caught a ride with a trucker across the Coeur D'Alene's up in Idaho and on into Spokane, Washington. Leaving Spokane, I got a ride with another trucker going to Seattle. He's, loaded with three hundred bales of hay, and when we reached Seattle, I helped to unload the hay. For my kindness, the trucker got me to Sumner.

Before leaving Salinas, Rayna had given me Jewel and Cam's address, just as if I ever got that far in my travels. Therefore, when I showed up at their door, Cam told me they had expected me after receiving a letter from Rayna, strongly suggesting my arrival shortly.

Within my first week in Sumner, Cam's brother Frog gets me a job at the High-Grade Meat Packing Company in the City of Tacoma. From there, the weeks flew by, as did everything concerning my lifestyle; that by now, had become very comfortable, including a Washington State Drivers License. Everything around me seemed to go well, and my only worry; getting drafted with the Vietnam War still going on.

However, no one could ever say that my life did not sometimes come without unexpected events and any explanation or warnings. Jewel and Cam did not possess a telephone in their home, and therefore they would walk down the street to a payphone when they needed to make a call; this is a dedicated weekly ritual for Jewel to call her family in Salinas. On one of those occasions, I walked down the hill with them, and while Jewel is talking on the phone, she mentions to Rayna that I was standing right alongside her; Rayna wanted to speak with me.

Rayna, "I'm pregnant!"

Who's the lucky Father?"

Rayna, "In fact, David and I need your help."

Rayna, "Sure, but what can I do?"

Rayna, "You know how Mom and Dad are; well, when they find out, "I am pregnant, and not being sure of who the Father is, Dad, for sure, will disown me. But if I tell them it's your baby, they might not take it so appalling because we dated for a long time, and the odds of us having sex would have been much greater in their eyes than some other boy."

Me, "I understand what you're saying, but I don't need to get caught up in your mess."

Rayna "Let me pass this on to you. The other night on television, President Kennedy said that any man married with his wife expecting would avoid the draft, and during the Vietnam War, not too many boys want to go in the first place, and that includes you. Both of us could benefit, I could face my family easier, and you avoid the Army."

My next decision is if I considered the outcome and years of hell it will bring, I would never have done it, and the draft would be like icing on a cake compared to what is coming down the road.

What drove my decision to take her up on her offer was when she said that I would avoid the draft by marrying her. Even my gut could not convince me not to marry her. After my dealings with Rayna, if there is one incident about her that stood out more than any other did, she was a pathological liar. That and that alone is why I had broken off with her. It truly is not because I caught her with Robby; I had only used that as an excuse.

Within two weeks from that phone call, Rayna had arrived in Sumner, and we were, married at the home of

Jewel and Cam. Now, I had a wife I certainly did not need or want and pregnant to boot with some other man's child. To add to my aggravation, Rayna continued her daily crying about wanting to go home to be with her mother and father until I get so sick and tired of hearing her, I agree to return to Salinas. Of course, what that did for me is Rayna could be with her parents, and I had to face whatever consequences may wait there for those unpaid traffic tickets.

After we settle in with Rayna's parents, I surrender to the Monterey County Sheriff's Office. Of course, now that I am locked up, I have to return to the Courtroom, and I get the same Judge who sentences me. He orders me to twenty-two days in his jail, twenty-two glorious days that I did not have to spend with Rayna.

While I am doing my time, she rented a small one-bedroom home on West Laurel Drive, known as Tortilla Flat. While in Jail, I realized should I break it off; I did not have anywhere to live, and that brought me to thinking maybe I needed to remain with her until I get back on my feet.

Like every sentence, they have a way of ending except living with Rayna. When I checked out of jail, I walked ten blocks to Cal and Mother's house. Upon entering, I was surprised to find David there. He had escaped from the Brigg and is hiding from the Military Police. He and Cal were completing the sale of his car to buy a bus ticket, with the destination being somewhere in the State of Maine. I visited for about an hour before Cal, and I took David to the bus station. Just as David is climbing the steps to enter the bus, he turned to me and said the strangest statement.

"Hay Rock, I only think it is right, I tell you, the kid. You know, the one Rayna is carrying; it's mine. Because I was in the Brigg and had no clue if I was ever getting out, Rayna came up to sucker you to play the father. Good luck, fool."

Is life repeating itself? It is what mother pulled on Bob when she had gotten pregnant by Francesco Stallone. I stood there, not knowing what to make of what David had just admitted. And before it registered, the bus was pulling out. Unfortunately, this leaves me unable to question him. Cal and I continued standing there until David's coach was out of sight, and then Cal drove me out to Rayna's house. When I walked in, I hugged her and then told her about my encounter with David and what he had to say to me about Rayna, and she said.

"Well, there is no secret there. You already knew that. Is there a problem?"

Living around Rayna is a living nightmare, with her being this pathological liar. I even considered signing up for Vietnam; it would have been much safer than living with her. However, I stuck it out, and soon I had rejoined the workforce and had become financially stable, which meant it is an adequate time for me to move out. I knew she did not want her parents to think she is not this perfect daughter, so the best I have been, threatened to tell them the truth about our marriage, knowing that would do the trick in opening the door for my departure. My plan worked, and I moved out of the house and in with a friend. When the baby is born, I am recorded on the birth certificate as being the father. Of course, I was not there, and that did not sit well with her mother, who immediately said I was blackballed out of their family, a family that I wanted no part. I took into consideration that Rayna's parents had no clue about the truth about their daughter.

I started working for Douglas Samuels, a used car dealer on North Main Street, as a 'Lot-Boy,' i.e., a person who kept the cars clean. In the back of the lot was a body and paint repair shop, run by a man named Rod. I would hang around the shop as much as I could to learn the body repair and paint business. While working there, I had made a deal with Douglas to purchase any car taken in as a trade-in that he did not feel is a vehicle worth reselling. I would buy it and then refurbish it, and Rod would paint it. My personal car was a 1957 Buick that I had customized by chopping the top, lowering it, then installing custom hub caps and paint.

Around this time, I befriended John, a Cab driver, and it is his only task to keep my Buick stuffed with girls. With Rayna out of the way, the party never lets up. If John and I were not dragging the Main or hanging out at one of Cal and Mother's parties, we were with Candy, Dolly, and Quennie. Other than that, five out of seven days a week, John and I worked by day and partied by night. I would spend a couple more years dragging the Main before I grew out of it.

The best time parties ended when I pulled into Mel's and ran into Rayna and heard about her hard times trying to make ends meet. Right off, I could see she's pregnant. Out of our conversation, she asked if I might consider coming back and living with her, at least until she gave birth; my gut went wild, trying to tell me to stay away. One would think I would say to her no. However, it just so happened that I was out of work due to partying too much, which led to no money to pay rent, and soon I had no place to live and had been sleeping in my Buick. Of course, she reminded me we were still married.

Since moving back to Salinas, I had not seen or heard from Father or Alma. As for Ronny, we parted ways over an argument about him, thinking I should treat Rayna with more respect. However, I am still associated with Cal and Mother; I had stopped my vengeance towards Cal. That did not mean, should he decide he wanted another beating, that I was more than happy to oblige.

One afternoon, mother called me from the Circus Room Bar on North Main Street and wanted me to stop by on the way home from work. I told her, I could only stay for one drink; why people say that when they know, seldom, they cannot consume only one, and here I am thinking, I will only have one for the road and stayed until I became so drunk, I could not leave the bar of my accord. One drink leads to another, then another, and I had just started building trouble when I call John. Now he, too, is on his way to the Circus Room. He shows up with Candy, Dolly, and Quennie; the last remembrance I had was, handing my car keys to John and leaving the bar, getting into the back seat, and passing out.

The following day, when I awoke, I lay in the back seat of my car. When I sat up, the first entity I noticed is John asleep in the front seat, and then looking out the front windshield, I could see a sign, 'Biggest Little City in the World?'

Instead of John taking me home, he had driven through the night to cross the California Stateline, and upon reaching Reno, Nevada, he found a parking lot to gain some sleep. I threw myself back on the rear seat, rubbed my face, and thought for a moment before reaching back over to the front to slap John across the side of his head to get his attention. He sprung up as if he had, been hit with a baseball bat, and when he looked for what had just bounced off his head, and he's looking right into my eyes.

Me, "John, wherein the hell, do you think we are?"

John, "I don't know where we are?

Me, "Well, John, we are in Reno, Nevada." John, what are we doing in Reno?"

John, "You tell me, what were you thinking? It is Reno John; we are in fricking Reno, Nevada. John, what are we doing here?"

John, "Let me see, the last I remember, you were saying you wanted me to drive you home, and you tossed me your keys, and Candy, Dolly, and Quennie were saying something about we should go to Reno. Where are they?"

Me, "I do not have a clue. When I woke up, only you were in the car.

Chapter 7: Death Was Hanging Around

We are in Reno now, and the question remained; how did John ever manage it all the way there considering he was as intoxicated as I? Here we were in a town of gambling, with little money between us, and I knew there is no way Rayna is, going to believe what had happened. Then, I did not want to hear her yelling with a headache I already had, so the next best idea was to get John and myself a cup of coffee. We walked into the Harrah's Casino, and just inside the Virginia Street entrance, there was a row of slot machines, where I put in money and pulled the handle; three bars line up, jackpot. Low and behold, if I did not try it again, and the same event happened, breakfast was on Harrah's.

The right thing to do would have been to take my winnings and head back to Salinas. However, what I was feeling was a freedom I had never felt before. Maybe it was being away from Rayna; well! Between John and me, there was no talk of returning home right away. However, we both knew if we were to stay in Nevada, we needed to find jobs, which takes us to find an employment office.

At the Employment Office, we located a woman sitting behind a desk, and she told us the Zephyr Cove Water District is hiring. Zephyr Cove is a mountain community on the East Shore of Lake Tahoe, at the six thousand, four-hundred-foot levels, and fifty-five miles from Reno. Therefore, up the hill and over the mountain, we went. Upon locating the Water Company and the man who is doing the hiring, he told us.

"We are colonizing a part of the National Forest, and it is the job of the Water Company to get water and sewer service up there. Therefore, should you be willing to dig trenches along the mountainside, you got a job."

Upon hearing what the job paid, we knew we would stay on for a while.

With my hangover subsiding, I am back to normal, and I got this strong feeling and thought it best to call Rayna, anticipating she would be mad as a hatter; I was right. As I tried to explain what had taken place, she just continued her normal bitching. Even after I told her about the job, she continued her rambling. I also thought I would say that I would return home when I got my first paycheck. However, nothing seemed to satisfy her, and I felt in actuality, I did not give a darn what she thought and hung up on her. When I told John of my conversation, he suggested maybe we could go on an adventure farther down the road when we tire of digging trenches.

Even though neither of us was twenty-one, we still could get into Casinos. It is in a Casino where the strangest incident happened. A woman came up to me assuming of all people I could have been mistaken for, the rock-in-roll singer, Elvis Presley.

I will learn down the road that the woman who mistook me for the singer would not be the first of many others who will also achieve the same mistake.

The work on the mountain continued for several months. Then the snow came that eventually caused the digging to stop. With that thought of traveling still on the back of our reviews, we confronted our employer, telling him of our departing plans. The following day, we checked out of the motel and jumped into my 1951 Pontiac, with its head of an Indian standing proudly on the front hood. We were now off on an adventure across America, and a month later, I turned twenty-one. We headed out with only my gut knowing our destiny.

We left Zephyr Cove and headed east on Highway 50, through Carson City, and by the time we stopped for the night, we were on highway 40, in Kremmling, Colorado. On South 6th Street, there was a restaurant where we hustled the food and two of its servers to spend the next two days until we felt it were time to move on. At least I had left those girls with the same sexual experiences, as taught to me by Candy, Dolly, and Quennie.

Leaving Kremmling, we headed east towards Denver. At highway 34 and 40 junctions, we ran through the Mountain National Park, only stopping for fuel in Estes Park. When we reached the town of Greeley, John bought a newspaper. In the employment section, a furniture store wanted day laborers. Upon arrival at the store, and were hired for the day. With the money we earned, we had enough to head into Southern Wyoming.

From Wyoming, we turned east, headed down highway 34, into Nebraska. In McCook, we heard at a fueling station that there is work on a farm in Pierre, South Dakota, bringing in the Corn crops.

Leaving McCook, we turn north on Highway 83, headed for South Dakota. At Vivian, we continued north on Highway 14, into Pierre. Unfortunately, we arrive at the farm too late to get the job, and by now, we are stone-broke and out of gasoline. What food we had, like bread, lunchmeat, and some cheese, is also gone? We got a bit of luck when the farmer called around to other farmers, trying to find us work; a farm clear across the State in Vermillion needed help. Of course, we still needed to get there. Through the grace of the farmer, he gave us a full tank of gasoline from his storage tanks, and his wife packed a food basket for our journey. That day two people left Pierre very humbled by the farmer and a wife's kindness.

We were back on highway 34, and on highway 34 and 81, we turned south. In Yankton, we took road 50 into Vermillion. John pulled into a long driveway leading up to the farmhouse, hoping the job is still there. Stopping in front of a two-story white farmhouse, out came its owner.

"Are you the guys from Pierre?"

John answered, "Yes, we are, sir."

"Well, the job's yours if you still want it."

We now have work; however, it would be another week before we saw our first paychecks. Until then, my car doubled as our sleeping quarters, and a maggot-infested jar of Miracle Whip Mayonnaise is our only source of protein. For the next four weeks, day after day, we brought in the corn from the fields. I drove the harvester, and John followed alongside in a truck that my equipment would fill with corn, destined for the silage tanks, placed around the farm.

When the job ended, we headed south to Sioux City, Iowa, where we continued south on highway 77. In Oakland, we took highway 75 to the Missouri Valley, where we caught highway 30, to a junction Farm Road 58, and followed it to Persia. There, we turned south on Highway 199 until we came upon a highway construction crew working on a new highway called Interstate 80. They had already paved halfway across Iowa, starting from the Nebraska Stateline.

John drove up to the crew office, and we went in asking for work; when we walked out, we were pavers. Mile after mile, the new Interstate moved along with twelve-hour days. Each day when the shift ended, we were, worn out. With the weekends being the only days off, we made the best of them by going to the many towns in the area, like Omaha, Atlantic, or Harlan. It is the town of Harlan, which we favored since it had several watering holes filled with corn-fed farm girls. Therefore, it became our pivot point, too, and from work. Eventually, we rented a motel room there and drove the distance each day to and from the job.

Then, with no warning, I awoke one morning with a high fever, and with it came the vomiting. I had some unknown ailment, and it decided it is, going to stay that way, unknown. It lasted several weeks, and during that period, I could have just as well died from the pain and fever that it has brought; even my Doctor could not understand, and therefore he did not know how one went about making it go away. Some unknown virus had entered my body and was giving me the fight of my life. The same issue happened years before, right after I had napped in a lounge chair out on the patio when I lived with Father and Alma. There was not a Doctor who could locate the problem. The older lady, who owned the motel, stepped forward with her ancient remedies. Thanks to her, I recovered; slowly, day by day, and soon, my strength came back. I fully recovered, and John and I decided not to go any further with the Interstate.

We went looking for work around Harlan and came upon Harlan Builders, a company that constructed Pole Barns and Harvester Storage Tanks. We were, hired and on our first day of reporting for work, did we get a surprise? Our thoughts of working somewhere in Harlan went literally to the wind when we are, loaded into a pickup truck, driven out to the airport, and then flown clear across the State to Fort Dodge.

We would build Pole Barns during the week, but we were flown back to Harlan after work on Fridays. In Harlan, while we were on one of our weekends, we meet Robin and Fondella, at the Scratch Pan Lounge, in the basement of the Chicken Hut Restaurant.

Every weekend we all would meet at the Scratch Pan, where the night started by entering a contest between us to see which one would be first to drink every drink on the drink menu board, hanging behind the bar. Our other favorite fun is to go out of town, to where the cereal grass grew, and everyone would get naked, and then, using the ears of the plants, to play many games.

On one of our weekends off, Robin asked John and me to move in with her and her Mother at their farmhouse;

Robin's father had passed away years earlier. We took her up on her offer and moved in. From then on, every weekend when we were home, it is a coin toss to see who sleeps with whom; John got Robin's mother. When one woman was in their period, there was always Fondella. Life was excellent, and sex was even better, not to mention money is faring.

After being gone so long, I had all but forgotten the word Salinas. However, like all good stuff, it has a way of not being so tasty after all, as John and I are about to find out. Iowa's winter had arrived, where the temperature plummets into the twenties and stays there for weeks. Building Pole Barns had just about become impossible, especially while trying to pound nails into frozen lumber. The job ended in the winter, but we had grown tired of the girls and wanted to move on; maybe Texas? We needed to find an excuse and found it came the Friday upon returning to Harlan. As usual, everyone had dinner at the Chicken Hut before heading downstairs. It is there were just as the four of us were getting ready to sit down at our table, Robin's mother joins. As she grabbed her chair, she said.

"Well, girls, have you told the Boy's the lovely news?"

John asked, "What good news?"

The mother turned her head, so she was looking directly into John's eyes and said.

"All three of us are pregnant."

John looked at me, and I am looking at the girls, and it is another quick look at one another, as the three women are looking straight at us for our input on the subject. At that point, John needed to use the restroom, and I joined him. From that restroom, it was easy to climb out of the window and run for the car where John jumped behind the wheel and started it; and in short order, we were heading south, and neither of us even looked back to see the lights of Harlan disappearing into the night.

We had not a clue where we were going. However, one factor was for sure, and we were heading south on Highway 71 towards Missouri's dark skies. By early morning light, we had reached the junction of 71 and highway 59 leading for the Oklahoma Stateline. When we reached the town of Miami, Oklahoma, we stopped for the night.

It was around one o'clock in the afternoon when we checked into the Miami Hotel. Both of us were exhausted and only thinking of sleep. However, on the way to our room, we passed right by the hotel's bar, and it had just opened for the day. We had one beer mixed with tomato juice, then another. By evening we had reached our body's limit; however, neither of us had the sense to stop drinking, just to get some rest. John asked the Bartender where there is a nightclub and is, told the best place is over in the town of Afton called the Supper Club. Afton is twenty-two miles from Miami, and my gut is telling me not to go.

We had been to the Club for an hour when John met a girl named Debbie. Two hours later, I had become hungry, and the problem is, the kitchen at the Supper Club was closed for the night. Therefore, I learn the only place open was back in Miami. Of course, John is not leaving his new girlfriend; therefore, I made the trip back.

There I found an all-night diner, and after having a belly full, fatigue is setting in. My only thought was to head for the hotel; however, I remember John is still at the Club. The longer I sat in the restaurant, the more tired I become. I felt the effects of exhaustion, yet I could not leave him without a way back to the hotel. All I would have had to do is to stay awake long enough to get back to him, even though my gut is continually letting me know it is a terrible idea and not to go.

I left the restaurant, and as I am pulling away from the curb, I have a hard time keeping my eyes open. The road ahead had become a bit blurred, and then, the worst incident that could happen happened. All I remembered of that night is, coming up on a bridge, seeing lights far up the road, in Afton. I knew I made it across the river bridge, and I knew I had continued down the road until my Pontiac collided with parked furniture trucks, lift-gate.

Opening my eyes, all I felt is, my blood running down my face and flashing lights are going around as if they are coming from within my head. People were all around me. They were looking to see if death visited their little town. Some stranger came over to the scene and started helping me out of the tangled mess by pulling me from the car and then putting me out on the ground.

Upon contact with the truck's hydraulic lift, it had ripped off the car's front end. How I ever missed the engine on its way back to the trunk is a pure miracle. Then there is that Indian hood ornament. As I came to my senses, the realization started taking place, and I jumped up from the ground with blood still flowing everywhere. Most of my cuts and gashes came from the windshield glass. Upon the first impact, the rest of my damaged body came from when I grabbed onto that hood ornament as the hood and the engine passed before me.

Of course, the local Police Officer is on hand with his questions. While that scene is taking place, John and

Debbie came driving up to the wreckage in her car. John sees the Pontiac, and he realizes it is I. That is when Debbie pulled over to the side of the street. John found me sitting in the rear seat of a Police car and came running over. I tried to explain to him what had just happened. However, even I am not sure and not to mention; if I had known John could have gotten a ride back to the Hotel through Debbie, the wreck would not have happened in the first place; or if I had only listened to my gut.

Because the Police Officer could smell alcohol on my breath, he takes me to jail in Miami. John tries to plead with the officer, but he is adamant about his duties. Because I only have ten dollars, and the fine is twenty-three, I have to stay in jail for a remaining term of thirteen days, earning a dollar a day until I fulfilled my obligation. Even John somehow got himself arrested that night for obstructing an officer's investigation while doing his duty; he, too, would spend time in jail.

We spent our 1965 Thanksgiving Day at the Miami, Oklahoma County Jail, listening over the intercom to some radio program from Nashville, Tennessee called the "Grand Ole Opry." I have no way of knowing then that this Opry and the City of Nashville would one day play an essential role in my life.

It is also while I am in Miami, where I turned twenty-one. When John and I fulfilled our obligation, waiting outside of is Debbie. John and I had no problem with coming up with where we were heading now; we returned to Salinas. Of course, John demanded that Debbie come along, a decision that creates its own journey.

John could not have picked a worse girlfriend; she was married and has the only car. That is the only reason that made any sense why we should take her. I questioned John about the consequences of traveling with a married woman whose husband worked for the United States Mail Service was hauling the mail via highway 40, the same road we were about to take.; I suggested we take a different route, and with that thought, we all got into Debbie's dilapidated 1956 Ford, and with her behind the wheel; we drove off, headed west, taking Highway 60.

Crossing western Oklahoma, the car's engine started knocking, and the farther down the road we had gotten, the louder it got; we were now approaching the Texas Stateline and coming up on the town named of all things; Miami, Texas. It's in Miami that the car came to a stop on a hill above the hamlet; however, we could cast it down into the town. Another problem was that none of us had enough money to fix it; even if we had, the old car was not worth fixing.

We abandoned the car and were about to thumb a ride. Then John noticed a pickup truck parked up the road, and sitting in it is an Indian. He and Debbie walked over to talk to him to see if he might give us a ride; after some negotiation with Debbie offering to provide him with oral sex, John and I hopped into the bed of the pickup while Debbie road up in the cab into Amarillo, Texas.

With what little money Debbie had, she had enough to pay for a run downed dive room hotel down by the stockyards. That night gets spent putting up with Debbie and John's copulating throughout the night.

We check-out of the hotel in the morning and walked to Highway 40, where we started thumbing a ride. A Station Wagon pulls up with the man behind the wheel, warring a black suit, black shirt, and white collar around his neck. Jonas was the name he gave, a Preacher for one of the Churches in Tucumcari, New Mexico, and for a good reason, I am not telling which one.

John and Debbie got into the back seat, and I took the first shotgun. As the miles would pass, the Preacher pursued a conversation about his life with his God. Listening to him, I could not help notice how many times he would glance into the rear-view mirror. Without me trying not to look too obvious, I turned to look towards the rear of the car, and it is no wonder the Preacher was checking the rearview mirror; in the back seat, John and Debbie, with have turned down the Station Wagon's car seats, were having intercourse. I felt it only a friendly gesture to apologize for my traveling companions. Strangely enough, the Preacher surprises me when he says.

"There is no reason for an apology; in fact, I was going to ask you how I can get it on with her?"

The look on my face is one of surprise.

"Well, Jonas, I don't know. However, I feel that could get arranged. Why don't you pull over, and we all can discuss it."

John, Debbie, and I discuss the possibility on the roadside, and then John got the Preacher into the conversation. When we returned to the car, the Preacher gets into the back seat with Debbie, and John takes the wheel as we continued into Tucumcari. Upon arrival, the Preacher invited us to spend the night at his home, which turned out to be an exciting evening.

The Preacher's Wife prepares dinner while their nineteen-year-old daughter played a few tunes on the family piano. When the evening entertainment ended, the

Preacher's wife passed a hat around that had these pieces of paper in it for a drawing to see who slept with whom.

Everyone headed to his or her assigned room for the night. John went to bed with the Preacher's wife, while I bedded down with the daughter. Debbie bedded down with the Preacher again. During that night, John and I exchange bed partners. Come morning, the daughter prepared an excellent breakfast, and afterward, we travelers said our goodbyes and headed out once again for highway 40.

Luck is on our side this morning when a semi-truck pulls over and gives us a ride as far as Clines, Corners. Twenty miles up the road, the driver pulled his rig over to the side of the road; both of us had enough of Debbie and John's urge to copulating in his sleeper, and the two lovers were put into the empty trailer.

Near Clines Corners junction of highway 40 and 285, the truck driver is turning north towards Santa Fé, New Mexico. He pulls his rig to the side of the road, lets the two lovebirds out, and then says his goodbyes.

Clines Corners is an Oasis in the desert where you could get food, lodging, refreshments, and the only fuel stop within 169 miles. Looking around, all I could see was the desert. Once again, there we were, back out on highway 40, thumbing a ride. Nightfall sets in, and still no luck; Of course, John and Debbie are thinking the desert at night was this romantic place with its stars overhead, so the two decide to have sex out on the warm asphalt. Their actions prompted me to walk further up the road to where there was a highway drain ditch, and that is where I settled down for the night, and before long, they showed up and settle in as well.

At daybreak, the first four cars pass; however, coming up the road was a School Bus; a bright yellow one and it approached and slowed and came to a stop alongside us. The driver opened the door and told us to get in that he was a Police Officer from Richmond, California, who had traveled to the State of Ohio to pick up a new bus for his school district and was returning to California via the southern route.

Already on the bus was another passenger, a fellow hitchhiker that turns out to be a blessing, since neither one of us had any money. Since John and I left town with Debbie, I learned she wasn't the brightest person on the planet and she would do anything to please John; so I asked him to nominate her to befriend the lone hitchhiker. She does precisely that and offers him sex in exchange for him paying for our motel rooms and food every time the bus stopped for fuel.

On our first day traveling on the bus, our driver has chosen Albuquerque, New Mexico, to spend the night. John and I waited outside our motel room until the hitchhiker and Debbie finished doing what she did best, and then we came into the room for the night. Debbie kept the hunger away as long as we remained on that bus, not to mention our nightly lodging every night we stopped. Even when the driver pulled up at some Truck Stop, Debbie unzipped him to assure everyone got refreshments.

"She was a real trooper."

We departed the bus in Salinas at the Market Street exit off Highway 101 and walked towards the Circus Room to retrieve John's car; he had parked it there the night we left for Reno.

John just knew his car would be gone. However, I knew if he had parked his car in the rear parking lot behind the bar, it would be there. When we walked into the Circus Room, we sat up at the bar as if we had never left, and all three of us ordered a drink on the cuff. Then Lou, the night bartender, came on duty. When he sees John, he says,

"John, you need to take your car home. We're tired of babysitting it."

John Jumper up and headed for the back door, and sure enough, his car was still there. The day Bartender Ernie used his car battery and jump-started the car, and we were off to drop me at my mother's house.

When we arrive, I got out of the car and said goodbye; I never see either of them again. Some months later, I ran into a friend of John who tells me John and Debbie had made wedding plans; they should have planned her divorce from her first husband. Apparently, at the altar, Debbie was there. However, John was a no-show. The last anybody heard from him, he went north to Newcastle, where his brother lived. Debbie had gotten a job as a housecleaner for the Author John Steinbeck, and in later days, she found her way back to her husband in Miami.

I walked into mother's kitchen, and it is as if I had never left; everything was as usual; I asked.

"How is everything going, mother?"

Mother, "Oh, about the same, your Rayna keeps coming around asking if I have heard from you."

As the day went on and with me having conversations with some of the other people I knew around town, the news spread like wildfire that I am back and staying over at Cal and Mother's house. I heard a knock at the front door, and when I answered, standing there is Rayna and the child she had while I am away, that made two children I am not the father, yet both were carrying my last name. The reasons and circumstances behind why I left that day with Rayna are not clear even to me; however, I remained living with her for three more years.

Chapter 8: kidnapped

I am now working in the hamlet of Spreckels for Spreckels Sugar Company. I was driving through an Onion field along Harkins Road on my way to work when I see out in the area are people following a machine that's harvesting Onions. Among those people are Cal and Mother; they were filling up gunny sacks with Onions that have fallen from the truck to sell them to some store back in town.

The following day, I went to their house to visit, and to my surprise, they had stopped drinking and were attending Alcoholics Anonymous. Mother mentioned they had been going out to the Onion fields to earn enough money to stay afloat. They were also picking up used furniture and selling it at auction houses.

When I thought of my half-brothers going hungry, I offered to fund Cal in a second-hand, combination auction house and consignment furniture business, since he is an excellent salesperson.

Cal rented a building on Market Street; it is not long before they were on their road to recovery. I would stop by occasionally to find out how they were getting along; of course, Cal never offers to pay me back; and I never would ask.

Rayna and I live in Virginia Circle; our house sat where the street made a left ninety-degree turn; if I'm standing in front of my house looking out towards the road, I can see anything or anyone coming and going. The significance of knowing about that view will reveal itself soon. I am still with Rayna, considering I despised her, and since there is no love between us, I spend many hours longing to be back out on that open road.

With sugar beets being a seasonal harvest when the season ended each year, and the sugar mill would close, I would find work in the countless packaging sheds around the area. In my search, I, being hired as a line mechanic for Alameda Frozen Foods, a Carrot packing company; I liked it so well that I never returned to Spreckels Sugar.

In my second year at Alameda Frozen Foods, when the Carrot harvest began, as the seasonal workers came in to work, one of them caught my eye. I could not take my eyes off her as she walked past me on her way to the processing conveyors; I knew she is the one by the butterflies in my stomach. She is beautiful, yet, not the type one usually sees in a Carrot shed.

Joan was her name, and she would come to work each night in tight blue jeans, with her brown hair hanging to her hips. She and I worked the swing shift, and it is during one of those shifts when our eyes locked, and it is not long after that when love is in the air, a strange love. We were always holding hands and kissing; however, never is there any sex.

Because we both were married and had doubts about cheating, our relationship continued each night only at work. The only other night we went out is on a dinner date when her husband is out of town. That dinner date destroys our relationship.

Several months into the relationship, Rayna finds a credit card receipt belonging to Joan on the floor of my Cadillac; it is when Joan had paid for the gasoline on our way to that candlelight dinner.

Rayna saw the address on the receipt and went over to Joan's house, where she confronts her and her husband. After that day, any relationship between Joan and me was over. She never returns to work, and the last time I ever heard of her, is when some co-worker told me she and her husband had moved to Arizona; she walked out of my life just as fast as she had come into it. The question is why Rayna had been so upset over Joan when she had been fricking every man that came along every chance she could behind my back.

However, the straw which broke the Camel's back all started the evening when Alameda Frozen Foods ran out of Carrots and shut down. I arrived home about two hours earlier than usual and found Rayna's younger sister babysitting Rayna's two children; I asked the sister about the whereabouts of Rayna, and I'm, told she went to the Farmers Market. Since I am home early, I drove the sister home. When I hear my gut telling me, we were at the car door, "Look to the street."

When I do, a Pontiac's headlights hit me right in the face as it approached the curve in front of the house. As the car slows to make the turn, it suddenly picked up speed and continued down the road; my gut again said.

"That car, something is not right, and it s connected to you."

As the car fades out of sight, I continue my plight, and after dropping the sister off, the children and I return to the house. Upon exiting the car, we had gotten as far as the back door when we heard a woman's voice screaming; it sounded like she was just down the street from the house. I started walking towards the sound, and when I reached the end of my driveway, I saw her running out of the dark, heading right towards me; it is Rayna yclling.

"I was kidnapped!"

I thought, "Kidnapped my Ass."

Right then, my gut said.

"You're right in not believing her; she's lying."

Yet she seemed hysterical enough to have been telling the truth. By now, she's clinging to me; I got a firm hold on her hand while directing her back to the house, hoping once there, she could make some sense of herself.

After she settled down, I got her to explain how three men of Mexican persuasion had kidnapped her.

The Sheriff arrived and started questioning her.

Rayna, "I left the house this evening to go to the Farmer's Market. I first drove over to my mother's and picked up my little sister and brought her back to the house to watch my kids; then, I headed to the market; upon arriving, I parked my car right in front and went in. On my way out, I notice a car parked right next to mine and it had three men sitting in it; however, I thought nothing of it at the time and continued to step into my car. Just then, two of the men jumped out of their car and dragged me back into their car, and pushed me into the back seat. The third man drove the car."

She described every graphic moment of how each one of them had their way with her. She said that after they were through raping her, they stopped the car and threw her out. When she got to her senses, she realized where she was, just down the street from her house.

How convenient, "my gut is thinking."

The Sheriff puts out an all-points bulletin for the three men, and a Sketch Artist arrives to draw three portraits according to her description. When the artist leaves, the Sheriff said.

"I will be back in touch."

Something about her story did not connect with three Mexicans kidnapping someone out on the plain site of a Farmers Market. I was getting the feeling my gut might be right; she is telling a whopper of a story. However, it was too early to know where truth meets fiction; therefore, I took my vacation since it was to be, taken weeks before.

She and I went to Oroville, where she could have some peace and tranquility, while the Sheriff looked for her abductors. We took the children over to their grandparents, where they would stay until we return.

Cal and Mother had moved to Oroville several months earlier after selling their store in Salinas and rented another building that once housed a Montgomery Ward Department Store. It, too, is a second-hand furniture store and auction house; Cal had also started a demolition company. Several blocks up the hill from their store is Orange Drive, where they had purchased a five-bedroom home, overlooking the Feather River?

My Grandparents had also moved to Oroville from Montana. They had retired from farming, leaving Ira to running the dairy business. Grandmother's blood condition, the one she had contracted years ago, had now taken its toll as well. She only has a few more months before she succumbs to the disease; mother will take care of her until then.

Each day after our usual morning routine of dressing, breakfast, and coffee, Rayna and I would head for the Feather River, where we would walk along its banks; we spoke little; not even holding hands. It is at the Fish Hatchery, where we would stop and sit on the rocks along the river, watching our shadows dancing on the water's edge. It is there; that Rayna told me how much she loved me and what a lucky girl she was to have a man like me, telling me it was like telling me a Monkey just climbed out of her Ass and it was Blue.

Other days, when we were not at the Hatchery, we would spend the warmth of the days rowing a boat on Lake Oroville, and come by nightfall; we would roast marshmallows along its bank and sit around the fire. During those moments, I found the time to contemplate the thought of what our marriage could have been; however, it was what it was. Setting by the nightly fire each night, I kept hearing coming out of her mouth pure bullshit of bedazzlement; she kept trying to be so giving, so loving, and even thoughtful, which I, for one, knew she didn't have any of those qualities within her.

As time has a way of doing, it was time to return home, and we said our goodbyes and were off down the road with my thoughts leaning towards the Sheriff and wondering if he had located those abductors. I also entertained the idea of wondering what Rayna was thinking since she had remained silent during the entire trip home.

It is late in the night when we arrived home, and therefore we left the children with their grandparents until morning. The following Monday, I returned to work; I am now on the day shift. One afternoon on my way home, I stopped by Leon's house, a long-time friend of Cal and mine who lived over on Abbott Street.

I was driving down Abbott Street, and was passing by a used car lot. If truth be told, I wasn't thinking of anything of importance, and there it was. The same car that I had seen going by my house the night Rayna was supposedly kidnapped; I knew it was the same car. So sure am I that further down the street, the more curious I became and pulled over to a telephone booth. I called the car lot to hear for myself who owned that car. The voice on the other end said the vehicle belonged to him; the man sounded damn familiar, and at once, I became sure whom it belonged; Robby, Rayna's old boyfriend. I then asked if the car was for sale, and the voice said no. By the time I got home that afternoon, I had decided not to mention what I had discovered; I still had more investigating to do. Or did I?

Later into the following day, around four, the Sheriff comes knocking on the door. I invited him in, and he makes this statement,

"I have three men in custody, and I wanted to have Rayna look at some mug shots hoping to identify them."

The Sheriff comes clean with me, telling me what had taken place the night of the alleged abduction. He also said he would arrest her if she identifies any of the men in custody.

Rayna entered the room, and the Sheriff gives her some mug shots. Lucky for her, she did not identify any of them. Then the Sheriff lays the hammer down.

Sheriff, "Would you like to change any of your original stories?"

Rayna, "No, why would I change anything?"

Sheriff, "You could go to jail for sticking to the ones you first told me."

Rayna, "What in the hell are you saying? I haven't lied!"

Sheriff, "Try this out! With your husband working nights, you never expected him to come home early. I do not believe there was any abduction here. I talked to a man named Robby, and he said that you were with him that night; the night you stated you were, abducted. It was Robby's car your husband had seen going by the house that night; what he did not know is it also had you in it. You were coming by the house during your date, ensuring everything is ok and finding your husband's home. Unfortunately for you, he had left work early that night. When you two saw him in the driveway, you panicked and concocted the abduction story. You went to the Farmer's Market, as you said, however, to meet Robby. As you were waiting for him to show up, you saw the three men parked next to you. That is how the story of the three men came about. I believe you planned; in case you were to be, caught, you concocted your story. You are a brilliant and cold, calculating woman."

The Sheriff asked her again if she would like to change her story, and she confesses to the charade. The Sheriff said to me.

Sheriff, "If she had identified the three men, she would have committed another crime far worse than cheating on you."

Because she already had two children to care for, the Sheriff did not arrest her. However, he had this to say to me.

Sheriff, "No man deserves a woman like you're married to."

He did not need to tell me something I already know, and I moved out of the house. To play me like that was more than I was going to accept. I was more than willing to rid myself of her before I did something to her I might come to regret. I had no second thought about her parents' dislike for me; however, I felt it about time they knew what kind of daughter they had raised, and despite my gut warnings, I am determined. I did not consider that she might have called them to give her version of the story just in case I came around telling the actual story, and that is just what I tried to do. At her parent's house at the back door, I'm met with a shotgun held by Rayna's father, and it's aiming at my head. Before I can say a word, he tells me to vacate his property at once. It only takes me a second to realize, as his daughter, trying to explain anything to the lunatic, was feudal, especially after years of me not coming forward about Rayna's behavior. Therefore, I respect the man's wishes with that gun at my head and leave his property.

After that fiasco, I wash my hands of Rayna and her family. I settle down to working hard; I was still working days, plus a few night shifts, picking up all the overtime I could. After that kidnapping ordeal, I am learning to pay very close attention to what my gut has to say. The next time I hear from my gut, it's letting me know my days in Salinas were numbered. I had not a clue about how this move was going to take place. However, what I knew, if the gut said it, then I am making some move. Until I got a game plan, I concentrate on work.

It is at a processing plant next door to Alameda Frozen Foods, where I met Donna. She was their United States Department of Agriculture Food Inspector, whom I had known for a couple of years. Frequently, I had run into her out on the town with Rayna. I would often notice her at the Five High Club or the Frontier Town Inn drinking and dancing. Over time, I had known her; we had shared loads of conversations. She would come over to Alameda Frozen Foods during her breaks when we both worked the swing shift. It is during one of those breaks that she invited me to have lunch with her. That first lunch began a nightly ritual that eventually turns into us having an affair. Secretly, we would share a bed far away from her husband, and as that affair continued, she tries to get a divorce; however, it had become an arduous task for having two children.

Many nights, while running the packaging machines at Alameda Frozen Foods, my thoughts drift far above the noise, people, conveyor belts, and daydreams of Donna. My nightmare was, knowing Rayna, and several other experiences I had already lived. And most of all, where was my future going?

Every swing shift had become a ritual. I watched bags of Carrots fall from out of the wrapping machine onto the conveyor belt as if they were enticing me to the wonder of their destination. I wished I could somehow follow along on their journey, far away from those immigrants, who filled the factory floor.

Like most Salinas companies, it depended on the seasonal crops to operate. Between crops, several companies closed down, and Alameda Frozen Food was no exception. When the season ended, the plant closed and would not reopen until the following season. I would continue working during the shutdown, getting all the equipment in shape and ready for the upcoming season. However, on my way to work one morning, the thought came to me.

"Should I take my vacation or work a few weeks longer?"

I was also pondering the thought of asking Donna to run off with me; after a good night's sleep the following day, I knew I was putting in for that vacation when I returned to work. As I drove into the parking lot that morning, to my surprise waiting, there is Rayna. She brought me the fantastic news that her father is, gunning for me. The reasoning for wanting to end my life is that her father thought I should pay child support, I told her.

"Why would I pay child support for children who are someone else's?"

That day in the parking lot, as she tells her story, I caught sight of her carrying a third child, another one not, fathered by me. One of my biggest mistakes is not getting a divorce as soon as we returned to Salinas just after we had gotten married. I knew it would be hard to convince anyone I am not the father, especially since I had never gotten that divorce. I thanked her for coming, then said goodbye, and headed to the human resource office to meet with my employer.

"Say, Mr. Summers, I'm taking my vacation."

Mr Summers, "Before we talk about your vacation, who's Tiny?"

Me, "He's my Father in law. Why?"

Mr. Summers, "He called the office and said he is, coming over here to kill you."

Me, "I heard."

Mr. Summers, "I don't believe you have long to wait."

Coming from outside, the two of us heard Tiny yelling my name.

Mr. Summers, "Get the hell out of my office, Hell, walk out of the building. I will prepare your vacation check, call me later. Someone call the police!"

I left the office, only to observe, Tiny walking towards me with that same shotgun I had once had at my head in his hand. He raised the gun and fired. I ducked behind a car for cover, and when I saw, Tiny trying to reload, I got up and ran like hell to my car, jumped in, started it, and drove out of the parking lot. The only way out was to pass right by him, and as I did, he started firing again and heard the buckshot hit the trunk of the car.

Tiny ran to his car and jumped in, and followed me through the City Streets. We traveled at unsafe speeds up north Sanborn Road, and I am feeling it is like the old days when I raced down the Main. We turned on Williams Road, heading to Old State Road. It is just plain damn luck someone had not gotten killed. I headed south on Old State Road, and with higher speeds, I finally lose Tiny, and after turning on Zabala Road, I came upon a row of Eucalyptus trees where I pulled under and waited until I felt it is safe to head back towards town.

When I return via Alisal Road, as I turned onto the East Alisal Street, Tiny parked about a block ahead of all people to spot. It is clear he also saw me as he pulled out onto the road and headed straight for me. It is a chicken race for sure, and as our cars came closer and closer to one another, the more determined I became at wanting to kill the Son-Of-A-Bitch by hitting him head-on. Just as our cars were about to collide, Tiny swerved out-of-the-way. And that puts him toward heading straight into a living room of someone's house. I skidded to a stop, backed up, got out of my car, went running over to Tiny, pulled him out of the vehicle to the ground, and beat him about his head just long enough until he was barely alive. I stopped. I then reached into his car, took his shotgun, smashed it over the opened driver's side door, then returned to my car and continued to my Cottage.

The morning of the next day, I went outside to glimpse at the damage from the buckshot. Seeing that is all I needed to convince myself, it is time to move out of

Salinas; again, my gut was right. Rayna came driving up to about then, and when I went up to her car, she hands me out of her window divorce papers to sign. She said her father is in intensive care. I replied.

"Good."

For the next two days, I spent most of it packing up at the Cottage. I spent my last two nights with Donna. The first night, besides making love, we discussed the various reasons she could not leave with me. I would have preferred to take her; however, I knew it is impossible with her being married, plus having the children. The last thing I needed is to take off across the country and have her husband report me for child kidnapping.

On the last night, she left in tears, hopeful I would return in a few months, and we could do whatever it took to be together. Her last words to me were,

"You know, Rocky, I can't live without you. I might just as well kill myself."

Of course, I laughed at such foolish talk and then assured her I would return as soon as I am, settled in somewhere.

Before I left town, I wanted to say goodbye to my friend Jack, who had moved to Salinas from Greenville, Mississippi, with his mother and sister after his father died.

Jack's brother also lived in Salinas and had been ever since he mustered out of the Army from the Fort Ord Military Base over in Seaside. Jack and I met the day he came to the Carrot Shed, looking for a job. After being hired, we befriended one another. When I arrived at Jack's house, his sister Annie's car is, parked in front. Soon after I entered the house, I learned she had been having marital problems, and for that reason, she was going to live with her grandmother, who lived in Baltimore, Maryland; she planned to take a Greyhound Bus. With what she is saying, I got to thinking that since I am leaving as well, I sure in the hell could have cared less where I went, and maybe she would consider having me drive her there.

Chapter 9: Bill &Mary

I had met Annie a week after meeting Jack. Even then, I could not deny her beauty, and I knew I would be a fool if I did not offer to drive her anywhere she wanted to go. Therefore, I provided her with my services primarily when it occurs to me.

"If I drive her to Maryland, it would not be far from there to my Aunt and Uncle's house in Northlake, Illinois, out in the west Chicago suburbs."

Annie agreed to have me take her to Baltimore, and we planned our trip, then I headed for Alameda Frozen Foods to retrieve my last check before heading back to the Cottage.

I have always had to live with strange things happening in my life, something that cannot ever be, planned with any assurance of the outcome. Here I had a high-quality job that held a future, yet fate had arbitrated and changes my menu. I did not know it then; I was about to head straight on into a lifestyle, one that had more twists and turns than a tornado. A lifestyle more complicated than any other growing into adulthood.

I was not just going to leave Salinas; I was leaving everything and everyone living there. However, I knew Rayna, other than my Step-Mother Alma, was the vilest person I had ever met, and with Rayna's children carrying my last name, she will use that to her advantage. I am not sure what she might try. However, I just knew I hadn't seen the last of her; therefore, I needed to make a plan to avoid what lurked within the dark boundaries of her already demented brain.

My first move was to apply for a different social security number? I checked into the law on name changing and learned that any person could use any name they chose and did not need a Court of Law to change it.

Our morning of departure had the Sun rising over the Diablo Mountain Range. It left more special than Annie did or I could have ever expected. Usually, Salinas had a cloudy overcast coming from the Pacific Ocean, but not this day. It is a beautiful June morning, one just as beautiful as Annie herself is. She is a very tall girl, right at six feet, with a 38-26-36 figure, to go with her naturally long blond hair. Her soft blue/green eyes seemed to have depth right into infinity. She had broken up with her husband over sexual matters, and I felt if she explained things, she had a few thousand miles to do so. Otherwise, I would not bring it up.

We headed for the car south on Highway 101. Reaching Paso Robles, I turned east on Highway 46 towards road 99 and then south again, heading for highway 58 at Bakersfield. That took us to Highway 40.

Over the years, though, I had always liked Annie and, as fate had chosen, here we were traveling companions. Out on the highway, we were telling jokes, stories and laughing into Kingman, Arizona. Coming into town, we checked into the Best Western on Route 40 Business, and by now, we had decided, one room would be all we would need, through to Baltimore; as I unloaded the car, she went inside the motel room to get her bath water ready.

With the car unloaded and her in the tub, I headed for the nearest grease-and-slop to gain hamburgers. Upon returning and upon opening the motel room door, there was a remarkable sight; she is standing there in the room with nothing on but a smile; those hamburgers were freezing by the time we ate them.

Leaving Kingman the following day, we were heading towards Albuquerque, New Mexico, hoping to get there by nightfall. Of course, I remembered that town all too well; it is there a few years earlier when the School Bus I am traveling on with John and Debbie stopped for the night. It is where Debbie had sex with a stranger, so we all would have food and shelter. Besides that memory, I am looking forward to taking Annie to Old Town for dinner; however, finding a motel is on our schedule.

Dinner is a success, and afterward, we walked around the town square, holding hands while stopping every so often to browse through the many shops along the way. After a couple of hours of walking, we were exhausted and returned to our room. When we hit the bed, both of us were expecting what is sure to come? The following day, we slept in, and by the time we departed, it will be hard to reach Oklahoma City by nightfall.

Passing through Tucumcari, I got to wondering if the Preacher and his family still lived there. Outside the town of Montoya, it rained and continued into Oklahoma City. The rain was in a flash flood category when we checked into a Motel 6. The rain continued its downpour right through the following day. After breakfast, we continued east, and it is not until we reached Wheatley, Arkansas, before the rain had let up; the next day at checkout, we headed for Nashville, Tennessee. The sky had finally become bright blue and clear. It will be late in the evening by the time we get there.

We check-in at the Roger Miller King of the Road Motor Inn; the following day, we decide to take in the local tourist attractions because Nashville is the Capital of Country Music. We visited Music Row over on Sixteenth Avenue, the Ryman Auditorium, the Parthenon, Belle Meade Plantation, and even took a tour of the Country Music Artist homes before ending our day down on Broadway Street where all the bars and record stores are.

As our time in Nashville ended, and once again, we were, headed eastbound. Arriving in Roanoke, Virginia, the sky is clear and full of stars. We checked into the

Coachman Inn, and since it is so late at night, the only place opened to find a bite to eat is a truck stop down the road.

After leaving the restaurant, we went back to the Inn and went out to the pool area, and we made love under the stars. Come early morning, as the earth brought the Sun up over the Blue Ridge Mountains, we were again back on the road.

Our travel adventure ended in Baltimore. I enjoyed the trip with my six-foot blond beauty. I spent a week with Annie and her Grandmother before moving on to Chicago; it had been, a week of passion that ends when we arrived.

Early one morning, as the sunlight from the east is warming up the countryside; I quietly opened the house's front door and pushed open the screen door with my suitcase ever so softly as not to awaken anyone. I step off the porch onto the sidewalk path leading to the front gate. There, I stopped a moment, sat down the suitcase, and just stood there looking back at the house. When I glanced up toward the morning sun, I could see that it had gotten even higher. I picked up my suitcase and continued down the sidewalk towards the front gate, knowing that there is no coming back to Annie once I opened it. As I continued walking, I kept looking over my shoulder to see if anyone is coming out of the house. To keep Annie's grandmother's dog "Dirt Bags" from barking, I had two large meaty bones that I had gotten from the butcher the day before. Dirt Bags was like any other dog; he would rather eat a first-rate old bone any day than waste his time barking. Passing through the front gate, I continued until I reached the car. I loaded my things, got in, started the engine, put the transmission in gear, and headed on down that dusty road, which eventually took me to the Windy City; I never came back to Annie.

I took Interstate 70 to connect with Interstate 80, heading west and right across the Illinois Stateline. I come upon wildflowers growing out in a pasture and pull to the side of the road to pick a handful of the beautiful colorful blossoms for my Aunt Mary upon my arrival. I am excited about seeing my Aunt and Uncle again. When I arrived in the town of Northlake, I immediately searched for their address. Upon finding the house, I parked right in front and walked up to the front door, and then knocked. Aunt Mary came to the door and has no clue that it is I standing there right in front of her, all grown up.

Mary, "Yes, may I help you?"

Me, "Aunt Mary, you don't remember me, I know?"

Before I can say another word, she looked into my eyes and said,

"Goodness, is it you, Rocky, so grown-up?"

She pushed the door open and gave me a massive hug as Uncle Bill comes to the door to see what all the excitement is about; he, too, is stunned by who it is. They invited me in, with both of them being the warmest two people as I had once remembered to be.

After the time to cover all the miles of memories and further plans, they invite me to stay with them, and of course, I took them up on it. Over the years, I had gained three cousins' two girls, Billy Joan and Sheryl, and one boy, Terry. Bill, Joan, and Terry had already moved away from home. The baby of the family, Sheryl, had grown up and had become this beautiful woman.

Breakfast in the morning was with Mary and Bill, and the conversation once again lent itself towards past years of exchanging more stories of the family; when finished, Bill and I retired to the front living room where I started looking for work in the local newspaper.

"Say, Uncle Bill, I see here in the newspaper that some company named Jewel Foods is hiring warehouse workers."

Bill explains who they are, and the following day after breakfast, with direction supplied through Bill, I am headed for Jewel Foods, a major grocery chain in and around Chicago land. It is going to be my first time using a new name and social security number. Of course, I only hope that I am the best-looking applicant applying that day with not having any work or educational history.

Well, I certainly must have been the best-looking person after all because that night at the house, the phone rang and when I answered it, the person on the other end of the line said I had gotten the job. He continued telling me how I had received very high marks from my last employer; I knew that was a lie. However, what I am hearing gives me a laugh because I had lied throughout the entire application. The man could not have checked with anyone because my last employer did not exist. Of course, the one thing I knew, 'the bigger the lie one tells, the more people who will believe you.'

I started the job on the graveyard shift. It required me to pull orders of case foods and placing them on a four-wheel flat dolly throughout the warehouse. Once I had filled a cart, I would hook it to an overhead chain conveyor that eventually winds up at a loading dock to be, uploaded onto a semi-truck headed for one of their retail stores. Then the process started all over again. After several weeks, I could see there is no chance of getting on the day shift, and I quit working for Jewel foods and applied at the Alberto Culver Company home of Alberto V-O5 hair products.

The position I applied for and am, hired for is a line mechanic. It is right up my alley since that had been my job title at Alameda Frozen Foods back in Salinas. When he comes to packaging machinery, I don't believe there is anyone on earth who better qualities more than I do.

During my stay in Windy City, I do not know how it happened. However, somehow Sheryl and I fall in love. We would go out every night, sit on the benches around the water pond around the corner from the house, or parked in her car somewhere making out, knowing it is wrong for first Cousins to be in this kind of relationship.

Of course, I was very much aware that it was only a short time before we had to stop; our love affair could not go on because it would lead to intercourse; if that happened, it would be too late to turn back. I may not have liked it, even though I had come up with every reason there is to tell me, it will work itself out; however, whom was I fooling? The relationship needed to stop, and the only way it was going to be if I left town. Therefore, I went back to Baltimore; however, I would not be seeing Annie. Of course, it is not my idea, and it's my gut.

What the hell was going on with my life, I was thinking? I up and leave Salinas, and that is strange enough. Taking Annie to Baltimore was just as puzzling. Now I'm living in Chicago, and all the while wondering why I am here? Then there is Sheryl; why her? Soon I am returning to Baltimore. The last time I am in Baltimore, I had taken a liking to the City. Therefore, it's the solution to my dilemma, and I quit Alberto Culver. I could hardly just break it off with Sheryl because there wasn't any reason to hurt her; therefore, I made up the story that Alberto Culver is transferring me.

It was four in the morning when my journey to Maryland started I left Aunt and Uncle a note instead of waking them up. I knew I should have told them the night before that I would leave that early. However, they were sleeping when I got home from being out with Sheryl, where we were saying our goodbyes.

I had a look out the front room window, and it looked as if Chicago land is in a snowstorm that had no mercy. I am thinking God must be mad at the Windy City with its miserable gray morning and streets that were becoming whiter by the minute.

Quietly, I entered Sheryl's room, and as she lay sleeping, I stood there looking down at her beauty with the thought that I must be senseless to be leaving the one I love. I pick up my suitcase and head for the house's front door and out into the cold.

Outside, I got the feeling of the wind chill from the blizzard. It must have been seventy-five degrees below zero. I truly believed all it did in Chicago land is snow to the point of freezing one's Ass off. As I started the car, the eight-track came on to the song by Simon and Garfunkel, "Homeward Bound," as I sat in the cold, freezing car waiting for its engine to pick up enough oil to move it on that ultra quite cold morning. When I pull out on the street, the car tires on my 1963 Pontiac sounded like they were rolling over broken glass. Of course, it does not stop me from getting to Interstate 80, the same highway I had once worked on back when I am twenty years old. My primary concern is hoping that the Interstate would become less icy. The snow has filled Chicago Streets in the City, causing a usual snarl, even at the early hour.

Like any other commuter in Chicago's morning traffic, I am a man on a racetrack, threading my way around the indifferent traffickers. They were, showing a low level of intelligence, as I am, for being out in a snowstorm. Even though driving is not a pleasurable task, I am determined to fight my way through, with all hopes of reaching the Interstate in one piece; I found the conditions here did not progress any better. Road visibility is terrible, causing me almost to miss the entrance to the on-ramp. Once I am on the snow-packed highway, I made it through Indiana, across Ohio, and a small part of Pennsylvania before the blizzard diminished. When I reached Maryland's Interstate 70 in Pennsylvania, the blizzard has turned into light rain.

I arrived in the City of Baltimore, and it had been some time since I first laid eyes on it. From the Internet 70, I took the 695 Beltway south, turned off onto the Baltimore National Pike, and then pulled into a filling station on Winters Bane. After talking to the duty attendant asking about finding somewhere in the area where it is clean and cheap to live, the man directed me towards the community of Brooklyn Park.

I got back on the Beltway and continued south and get off onto Ritchie Highway. At Ease Patapsco Avenue, I turned right and again on Pennington Avenue. There I started driving up and down the many Row Houses that dominated the area, hoping to see a "For-Rent" sign attached to one. I had not been searching long when I went down Sycamore Street and caught in a window, "Furnished Apartment for rent." I paid for the first month and then started unloading the contents of my car.

Within an hour, I had somewhat settled in and took off for a walk around the neighborhood. I walked up Sycamore Street and turned right on Fairhaven Avenue. I continued to Sassafras Street, where I turned right again. It is at Sassafras and Pennington Avenue, where I came to a neighborhood bar. As I entered, I noticed its patrons looking at me; at first, I had no clue why. Then, I realized; they must have wondered whom this stranger walking in their bar?

However, that is not the case. By this time in my life, I had morphed into looking like a twin to rock-in-roll singer Elvis Presley; what they were starring at, they thought Elvis had just come into their bar; at least, that's what people had told once we befriended one another.

I became the center of everyone's attention. Over by the restrooms, at the back of the place, was sitting my new landlord with another older adult. For the first time, an entire bar full of strangers picked me out of a crowd and tagged me against Elvis, and because of their mistaken identity, I could not buy a drink. Everything is free. At closing time, I walked back to my apartment; however, I am not alone.

The following day, upon looking at a daily newspaper, I luck out finding several jobs to apply. I chose the ad asking for a line mechanic, experienced in repairing packaging machinery, at the John D Copanos Pharmaceutical, manufacture of Penicillin. In the personnel office, I received an application and a meeting with the personnel manager, who never checked my background. The man asked the pertinent questions, and I supplied the answers and got hired.

Chapter 10: Donna

When the interview is over, I headed back to the apartment. When I got out of the car, I noticed a girl sitting on her front stoop across the street. I walked over to introduce myself; however, I got surprised when she already knew all about me. I just stood there a moment staring at her, and then I said.

"Damn, well, it is a pleasure to meet you. Say, I'm going over to the corner bar for a drink; why not come with me, since you already know all about me?"

Her name is Windy, who is a lesbian that later on, that night, invites me over to her apartment to join in some fun and frolic with her other three roommates. Being the humble man I am, I somehow made it through that night.

Just about every night after the first, I am hanging out at the corner bar, and there I befriend Brian, the bartender, and his brother Danny, the bouncer, and as our friendship grew, so did my/Elvis popularity. Looking like Elvis was all it required. I am being made the guest of honor at the corner bar every night, and only on my looks and the people's mindset that they were looking at Elvis; it took me on a completely unique life path than I could have imagined.

Brian was dating a hooker who worked on the "Block," a stretch on the 400 blocks of East Baltimore Street in Baltimore, containing several strip clubs, sex shops, and other adult entertainment merchants. After knowing the two brothers for a month, the three of us, after the bar closed, would go across town to the Block.

One evening I called Kenny to let him know where I am, and to my surprise, he surprised me when he said it just so happens; you are living on my old stomping ground. He told me there were a couple of old friends he sure wished he could introduce to me. I suggested he fly out to Baltimore, and within a week, Kenny has arrived. We visited all of his old haunts, and I am, introduced to more Mechanics' than I could have ever thought were in the area. One of those Mechanics was Garret, or maybe more than a Mechanic; He is an architect, and that meant there is no better if one wanted someone to disappear, and for the rest of Kenny's visit, the three of us became inseparable.

Months after Kenny returns to Salinas, Garret introduces me to Venny (the pimp) Tortello, who at the time of our introduction was heading to prison on a narcotics charge and needed somebody to take over his territory until he returned. The girls who were working for Venny started working for me. It was not long before the girls were known as the Elvis Girls. They received twenty-five percent per trick, paying me seventy-five percent for bookings, protection, and executive limousine service to and from the safe house in Federal Hill, a neighborhood named for a prominent hill that viewed from Baltimore's Inner Harbor. I would take Venny's twenty-five percent off my percentage to a bank deposit box so he would have plenty of cash when he got out of prison.

In time, I had moved the girls to the Washington, D.C. area. They worked the diplomatic circuit there and between Government Officials in and around the Baltimore area; soon, the Elvis Girls had become famous as far as New York, to the De Wallen Red-Light District in Amsterdam, and into the Angeles City in the Philippines. I am supplying the best hookers that money could buy. For an hour with one of the Elvis girls, her companion paid as much as two-thousand dollars, depending on what he wanted; no girl got less than one-thousand dollars per trek. In keeping a low profile, I moved out of the apartment house and into Brian and Danny's three-bedroom, just about four miles from the corner bar.

One evening, I called Jack in Salinas and learn from him that Annie had reconciled with her husband, and they were living with her grandmother. When I asked about Donna, Jack said she had tried several times to commit suicide, and that brought me to remember that she had suggested once of doing just that; should I not return to her? That bit of news got me thinking that I needed to make a trip to Salinas as I had promised.

Using Venny's Lear Jet, we landed at the Monterey Regional Airport in California; it was four o'clock in the afternoon when I rented a car and started the drive for

Salinas and on my way; I remember Donna liked yellow Roses, and with passing a flower shop, I stopped and purchased a dozen.

Arriving, I drove across town to where she lived, and when I came on her street, nothing had changed. She and her husband's cars were in the driveway; this confirmed she is still with him.

Seeing the cars got me wondering if her husband still worked for Bud Antle lettuce and on the night shift; if that be true, he would leave in a short while for work.

If he leaves, I needed to follow him to make sure that is where he is going. My wait was worth it, and I followed him, and sure enough, he heads straight to work. I turned my car around and headed back to Donna's. By now, Salinas is in total darkness as I am gathering up the Roses, closing the car door, and crossing the street and up to her door where I knocked. I could hear music coming from inside, and the lights were on with getting no answer. I walked around the house to the kitchen window to see if I could see anyone. I saw Donna with her head sticking in the oven. My first thought was to get in the house and I went back to the front door and found it unlocked; I opened it and headed straight to the kitchen where I smelled the potent smell of rotten eggs. I reached for her and pulled her out and put her on the kitchen floor. I was too late; she was already dead. A rush of cold chills came over me as I closed off the gas.

She kept to her words when she said if I did not come back, she would commit suicide. Now the question I would carry for the rest of my life; did she kill herself because she really could not live without me?

I sat on the floor, holding her in my arms as tears fell. I then carried her to her bedroom and laid her on her bed, and then I went back to the kitchen to retrieve the Roses from the floor. When I returned, I placed a few long stem Roses in her hand and then gently kissed her goodbye for the last time.

At that moment, a thought came to me; where were her children? I started a search throughout the house, and it led to another bedroom, which is where I found them; they too were dead, and by the looks on their faces, it is not from inhalation, more like suffocation. Of course, I had no clue about the reasoning behind the deed; however, I was not hanging around to find out. I placed a few more Roses in each of the children's hands and returned to Donna's room, thinking somehow maybe she is just asleep. However, there was no doubt she was, gone. I knew I had better get out of there before someone came around. I locked the front door and placed the remaining Roses on the stoop. While walking back to my car, I could not hold back the tears.

I went looking for Jack to tell him about Donna and told him how I had found her and the children. He reassured me she had not committed suicide because I never returned, and the fact I had been gone a long while, and if she had a problem with me not responding, she would have been dead long ago.

Other news was Rayna was now living off welfare, and to get on it, she had told the Welfare Office that I had deserted her and the kids, and she did not know where I am. However, the Salinas District Attorney had put out a warrant for me. I told Jack.

"Well, Jack, I had expected Rayna to pull something and had made, arrangements so no one could find me. Life is a strange bedfellow man."

I had nothing to do with getting her pregnant, yet they're looking for me. I returned to Baltimore and started focusing on business, and one added attraction, I started entertaining every night as an Elvis Presley impersonator. It began as a lark over a drinking, Cocaine snorting party in the club. The Elvis Girls had talked me into doing the act on the stage that night, and it went off so well that I started doing the bill on the strip club nightly. The girls become my backup singers, and every night we closed the show to a standing ovation. However, those days soon ended as fast as they had started.

Venny gets out of prison, and the way I had organized the business structure, turning the girls back over to him, took place as smoothly as possible; I had brought the business into the world marketplace. Of course, Venny insisted, I keep thirty percent of the future market for two more years.

Now that I am back in the ordinary world, I date a girl named Gail, and she had three children; I knew very well never to get involved with a girl with so much baggage; even my gut warned me of it. To add to the bags she already had, she was married. However, he was in County Jail on drug charges.

I call mother and learn that the draft board in Salinas has been looking for me for three months, wanting me to take my Army physical. As soon as our call ended, I called the draft board to explain I had not been dodging them; I moved to Baltimore. I'm told to contact the draft board there. And I'm to report to a facility in Dundalk where I would be tested and taking my physical.

I am excited about the idea of maybe getting drafted. For a long time, I could not practice my Mechanic skills and was better than being in the Army, where I could home in on my sniper skills and the chance of killing the enemy legally and adequately.

I took the physical and the paper test, and when I finished, I'm told they would be in touch with me within the next two weeks, and I would receive my orders where to report for duty. True to their word, I received the promised letter; however, it stated I had passed the age to be, drafted; I am disappointed.

The soap opera never stopped; Gail brings me the news that her husband is getting out of jail soon, and she is afraid of him coming around her and the children. While contemplating how to handle the situation, I call mother again to tell her what happened with the draft board. She told me she was opening a restaurant in Oroville and suggested I come out and help with the remodel if I had nothing better to do. I told her about what is happening with Gail's problem, and she suggested I bring her and the children out to California. Within a couple of days, we were packing for the trip. The only other person I told where we are going is Garret.

The trip seemed to be a long one; however, we made it to Oroville. I pulled up in front of Cal and Mother's house with the horn blasting. Out came Cal, Melvin, Ricky, and

Mother to see what looked like orphans getting out of the car. With the family's excitement over, we all went into the house, where we all grabbed a seat and caught up on family news.

Across the street from the Bazaar is the Oroville Inn; it is the only high-rise hotel in the area. It had been there since the days of the California gold rush. Roy Greyly and his wife Gloria ran the place; however, Roy spent most of his time over at the Bazaar, and there is where he and I met; He would come over for coffee every morning. One morning, Roy offered Gale and me a job at the Inn while the remodeling is going on over at the restaurant. We accepted and moved into one of the enormous suites, large enough to accommodate five people.

Gale worked the front desk during the day while the children were in school. I work the front desk on the graveyard shift, and during the day, I would help my Uncle Howard, who came up from Valle Vista, to help with the remodel of the new soon to be "Sylvia's Dixie Bar-B-Q," on Montgomery Street; one block north, of the Inn and the Bazaar Store.

Howard continued to drive up from Hayward, California, every weekend to help with the remodel of what once was a hamburger and fries place. Finally, the day arrived when Sylvia's Dixie Bar-B-Q is, finished. Mother now prepared for the opening day, and I quit my job at the Inn to start full time at the restaurant.

Out behind "Sylvia's Dixie Bar-B-Q" is the town's levee; it held back the Feather River from overrunning its banks and flooding the city during the spring runoffs when the snow melted higher in the mountains. All along the top of the levee is a gravel road that runs the entire length of the downtown area. After "Sylvia's Dixie Bar-B-Q" opened, grandfather, every day took his walk along the levee pass the Bazaar exit and continued walking until he reached the restaurant. There he would come to visit awhile and having a snack while telling stories of his Candle Light Café days before heading back to his home. Seeing my grandfather every day was a rare moment, considering I had only spent limited time with him since I had left Niles.

Sylvia's Dixie Bar-B-Q catered to the town's folk, however, not to the high school kids. With mother's dislike towards children, she refused to handle Hamburgers, Hot Dogs, or French fries. Her restaurant was a specialty restaurant, which served only Barbecued Roast Beef on a long French Roll, with a side order of Coleslaw, and Beans.

Business was steady; however, that is not what mother had in mind, a stable company. Each day, after the noon rush, she is in the back room where she sat for hours, drinking beer and smoking marijuana. One day after smoking, she came out and told me she is closing the doors; the doors closed one week later.

For the time, she was open; Cal did not have anyone to monitor him; therefore, he started drinking and smoking marijuana and taking Yellow Jackets; known as speed, and every so often, you could smell alcohol on his breath. It caused me to take over the Bazaar and Cal's construction company, which the City of Oroville chose when they wanted a condemned property in town demolished. Every day, Cal is hanging out with his car-racing friend Blake and drinking and doing drugs.

Between mother's rebellion over cal's plight and the constant daily battles between them, I felt the urge to move on. Gail's husband does not get granted parole after all, and that cleared the way to return to Baltimore. I called Garret, who has set up an all-purpose Collection Agency; for a better word. I tell him I am coming back, and he tells me he has several Client Contracts to fulfill and could use my help to get them fulfilled. I told him, sure. However, I would need a cover job, and Garret assures me I had one covered by a friend of his working at the Food Fair Grocery Chain.

We packed for the return trip; however, joining us is Brother Melvin because he was getting too hot for him selling drugs in Oroville. When we arrived in Baltimore, our first stop was in Woodlawn, where Garret had rented us a furnished apartment. After everyone is, settled in, I went to meet with him, and we drove over to the Food Fair Maintenance Office. Within a few weeks, I had gotten Melvin a job with the same chain as a baker's helper in one of their stores.

I spend the next two years working from eight to five and fulfilling contracts with Garret. One day Melvin tells me he wanted to move back to Oroville, and I got the idea I would take him there. Gale and I would make a vacation out of driving him back there by traveling the sightseeing route. We leave her children with their grandmother.

Our trip would take us through the Bad Lands of South Dakota, to Mt. Rushmore and down the Oregon coast, over Mt. Shasta, and finally, Oroville. When we arrived, we found Cal and Mother had been drinking for some time; Long enough to lose the Bazaar, Construction business, and it looked as if it would not be long before they lost their home to taxes.

On our second day in town, mother told me she and cal were heading for Las Vegas, thinking they could find work there. I told her I would follow them as far as Las Vegas before turning east headed back towards Baltimore. At the early morning light, we all loaded into our cars and headed out for Sin City. It is a small convoy, with Gail and I in the lead car, Cal and Mother behind pulling a utility trailer, and Melvin, Ricky, and some friend of theirs were trailing.

It was late afternoon when we arrived in the sun's city that is, surrounded by burning sand and gusting wind of hell's fury; a City in a neon oasis where a person could imagine dreams of wealth beyond one's comprehension.

Our first-night commendations were Kampgrounds of America, with life in the desert starting with Cal setting up a tent; a useless task because of the high wind that filled the air with sand. The sand was beating down as if one is standing in front of a sandblaster; it is swirling, blasting, and covering everything and everyone. Gale and I made our sleeping quarters in our car; as we were sitting in it, we watched the fiasco of Cal trying to set up the tent. Suddenly, through the swirling darkening sky, something came, flying past us. The wind had picked up their tent and hurled it into the air before letting down against a Motor Home. I ran to the tent; luckily, no one had gotten hurt. Mother was in it when the wind pitched it into the air, and she is yelling to get her out of the damn thing. All became well after everyone gathered their senses, and it is back to set up; this time, Cal did not forget to tie the tent to the tent stakes.

The next thing on our list is to find a place to eat. Mother suggested the International Hilton, and since we would go there, she suggested I dress somewhat to look like Elvis because she had heard he had played there. I thought.

"What does she mean; I already look like the man."

Well, I am totally against it; what would be the odds that anyone in Vegas would mistake me for being anybody else other than myself? Of course, I had never been to Vegas before and had no clue how people thought.

Everyone loaded into Cal's car and it's off to the International Hilton. Cal pulled into the parking lot, and everyone gets out, preparing to walk up to the main entrance. We were almost to the front doors when Presley's fans spotted me and came storming over, and if that did not scare the crap out of us, I took off running to get inside the Casino with those fans following; I headed for Security. By the time the fans caught up with me, I am safe inside the Security office. Even Security thought me to be Elvis at first and was going to do their best to protect me.

It is there in the security office that Security realizes they had only assumed I am Elvis. All involve getting a big laugh out of the ordeal when they find out I wasn't. From the crazy reaction coming from Elvis fans. Casino Security knows there is no way my entourage will get from their office and into the Casino restaurant on our own; therefore, they escort us there. As we were walking along, people were pointing and staring. However, Security made sure and everyone kept his or her distance.

It is the first time I had ever seen the inside of a Casino. I am amazed at all the glitter and glamor; it got me thinking, maybe entertainment is my forte after all, and right there, in that Casino, is where I started thinking of a way to get into that business; not having a clue it was my destiny. Once we are seated, we all got a taste of what the real Elvis must have to go through every time he's in public. People were coming up to me by the dozens asking for an autograph. Melvin and Ricky were acting as bodyguards with Security to keep the fans at bay.

What no one had noticed, nor did Security tell us that appearing at the Hilton is the man himself. Here I am; only a mirror image of the man and the people are all over me. The dilemma is how do I go about convincing people I am not the King? I tried telling people.

"I am not Elvis."

I turned to Security for the answer, and they said,

"Give them an autograph."

I knew by experience that if I signed with some sloppy flare, no one would be the wiser. Therefore, I signed and continued signing stuff for the next hour and never looked up; mother is trying to get my attention during all the commotion. She is trying to say something. However, I kept signing until a hand filled with diamond rings appeared on the table. This hand is not holding the usual. Whatever it is, they wanted to be approved. I glance up from the side, and as I did, I am looking face to face with the King of Rock-In-Roll; my heart skipped a beat, and my entire body turned beet red when the King said.

"Hey man, I have always wanted to meet you."

I just knew I am in deep crap.

"I am just having a little fun, Sir. I promise, I never signed your name!"

Elvis kept looking down at me while his bodyguards were holding the fans back, and he said.

"Son, there's only one King. You have got guts."

I replied, "I am just having a little fun, Sir. Was, not meaning any disrespect, and had, no idea you were in the Casino, I hope you are not too mad? My name is Rocky.

Elvis, "Well, I will give you this; you sure look like me. Maybe we are related?"

"Yes, sir, one never knows. I could be a cousin of yours if my looks say anything."

Elvis, "Well, Mr. Rocky, you need to stick around, and after my show, we'll get together and talk."

I reply, "Sure, man."

Elvis, "I'll tell you what, son. If you will stop being me, I will let you see my show.

"You got it. '

With that said, the two of us started laughing. However, I am a very nervous person. One of Elvis's bodyguards butted in and said something to the King, and he turned away to have a conversation, then turned back and said.

"I have a show in a few minutes."

Then he looked around the table and then spoke again.

"You all are my guests."

Chapter 11: The Tornado

That conversation at that table would last several minutes more before Elvis left, and as he does, he tells Security to get my group the hell out of the restaurant and into the showroom. I am sure relieved that the King was as nice as he was. We all got up from our table, and with our escort; we are on our way to the Celebrity Room,

For the next few days, Cal and Mother would go over to the Frontier Casino on Fremont Street every day to meet a country singer named Ferlin Husky, a long-time friend of Cal's. When it is time for Gail and me to leave Las Vegas, we said goodbye to the family and headed for Baltimore. The rest of my family headed for Jean Nevada, a town just west of Las Vegas, where Cal had landed a job as a Bartender at a Truck Stop Casino.

Upon returning home, I quit Food Fair and went to work for Sigmister Saw Company in Hillside, NJ as a Service Technician who delivered and repaired meat-cutting equipment throughout Washington, D.C., Virginia, West Virginia, Pennsylvania, and Maryland.

Among my many stops was the kitchen at the White House? Once a month, I would arrive in the kitchen early in the morning. One morning, I meet the United States President while exchanging all the dull meat-cutting knives for sharper ones as Secret Service looked on.

Other service stops took me to every Military facility in the D.C. area where I am meeting Generals and Admirals, to the places where the House of Representatives dined. Daily, at one point or another, I had met just about every politician in Washington, D.C., even the ones who paid for my Elvis girls back in the day; I always marveled at how I can have a security clearance. However, I might not have should they have if known about Garret and our business.

Most of my free time I spend doing jobs with Garret for our best Client, Venny. Once a month, I would cross the Battlefields of Gettysburg, Valley Forge, continue through the Amish country, and up through Camp David. I remained with the company for another couple of years.

Since I left Salinas, I have gone from being a machine mechanic at a Carrot Shed. A stock boy, a line mechanic, a maintenance man, a pimp, befriends a mechanic, impersonates, and meets Elvis Presley, became a Service Representative, and meets the President. Now Garret and I are getting ready to expand internationally.

I now devote my time building the business Garret and I started. And we have a big contract to fulfill that will be timely because of the many places we must cover; Kansas City, Saint Louis, and Reno, Nevada. Servicing these Cities and keeping a low profile, I would be on a camping trip with Gail and her children. Garret would arrive in the designated towns before I came doing recon.

When we arrived in Reno, we set up our campsite east of town at a campground along the Truckee River in Verdi, Nevada. It is there where I awoke one morning. No sooner had I walked out of my tent did I notice that in the campsite next to me, there is a Corvette parked. I walked over to the car, and by looking through the driver's side window, to my surprise, my half-brother Melvin is tucked in a sleeping bag; I knocked on the car window, Melvin opens his eyes. The first person he sees looking back at him is I. The odds of us being there in the same campground would defy any Casino odds. After our conversation about all people to run into, we sat around the morning campfire. Melvin said he had left Cal, Mother, and Ricky in Jean, Nevada, and had returned to Oroville. There, he restored his Corvette and needed a new frame for it and located one in Reno. Nearing the Verdi exit, he had seen the campground sign, and it was late in the night, so he pulled into it to get some sleep; however, the odds of ever again parking next to a brother that I thought is in Baltimore was another trillion to one shot. I started a fire and cooked a campfire breakfast and then Melvin said goodbye and headed out of the campground.

While waiting for Garret to arrive, the family and I spent days doing what campers do. Now, with doing the work Garret and I am doing, having a woman around is severe enough. And one with three kids is out of the question, and I am thinking of how to end the relationship, luck, fate, or whatever. Gale calls her mother and learns she is in ill health and needs her daughter home, and I have to take her and the kids to the airport. I stood out on the tarmac, watching her plane fly into infinity. It would be our last time together.

Garret arrived and said our client had gotten me a job at the Nugget Casino in Sparks, a community connected to Reno on its east side. The position is the bar Back, i.e., a person who brought all the ice to the Casino bars. Then cut up all the fruit for the cocktails, and cleaned up around the bar. The idea is with having that job; I could keep the surveillance on one particular Bartender until Garret went to take care of business in Hamilton, in Ontario, Canada, for another Client and then would return.

As I am still living in the campground, one morning, there is a surprise waiting for me when I came out of my tent. Melvin had called Cal and Mother and shared with them where I am. That prompts Cal to quit his job, and they head for the campground. With a camper shell on the back of their pickup truck, they were at home no matter where they were. All they needed to hear was where I am living; in a campground, and with that being right up their alley, they came to stay awhile.

For the first week, if they were not sitting out by the river drinking, they were in their camper passed out. Before long, the drunks had started their usual bickering with Cal slapping Mother around; the man should have realized who is, camped next to him. I took as much as I was going to, and a fight breaks out where Cal got his Ass kicked all over that campground. When I felt he had enough, I gave him some more beating and then politely showed him the way out of the campsites. With Cal gone, it causes Mother to living in my tent, and because of it, we were ready to find new lodging.

Way up high on a mountain above Reno was the La Questa Apartments on Skyline Boulevard, and when Mother saw the view, she had to live there. Our new two-bedroom apartment overlooked the town far off below the mountain. Within days of our move, Mother had stopped drinking and had found a job at the Prima Donna Casino in downtown Reno.

Everything is going well until the night Cal showed up at my job, inquiring into the whereabouts of mother. Instead of getting the answer he was looking to hear, I explained to him the advantage of getting lost. Instead of him leaving the Casino, he's plays cards and drinking beer.

By now, I am, promoted to shift Bartender. Every time the cocktail server assigned to my bar came to me to get Cal another beer, I would pour half of the beer out and replace it with Vodka. It is not long before he falls out of his chair, and Security throws him out. Not knowing what I was up to, Cal came back night after night and kept getting Vodka in his beer, and Security kept throwing him out. The day Garret returned from Canada, he made sure Cal left town.

Every weekend at the Casino, a new entertainer would headline. Usually, after their show, they would find their way to the back bar for that last cocktail of the night. The entertainers, who wanted to have a private party, away from the Casino and out of public eyes, would party with Garret and me. There were many parties at my place late nights up on the mountain where sometimes I did my Elvis act.

The Clubhouse at the apartment complex is plush and oversized and surrounded by glass, and anywhere in the room, one could look; they saw the lights of Reno down below the mountain, through the black starry night sky.

The last party thrown there is with the performer and comedian, Donald O' Connor, and his backup singers, the Doodle Town Pipers, and other cast members. The band that supplied the music is from Nashville North, a Reno country music nightclub.

Donald showed up with another performer. He is working the room at the Harrah's Casino, named Jim Neighbors, who tried putting the make on me, and the only reason the man is, left alive is that Donald asking me to overlook his friend.

Garett's and my commitments have gotten completed in Reno, and Clients have summoned us to Nashville, Tennessee. It is a good thing we left when we did because, on my last night, a process server came up to me at work and served me some papers. They were from the Nevada Department of Child Support, on behalf of the Salinas Department of Child Support.

What has happened? While I am working my shift, one of Rayna's old boyfriends named Harley had seen me, and after returning to Salinas, he told Rayna, and she told Child Support? I had twenty-eight days to report to the District Attorney's office to explain why I had not paid support. Twenty-eight days gave me the time needed to pack up and head east. By now, I added to my portfolio the title of an official Mixologist. Melvin and Ricky have been staying with me at the apartment, and with hearing I am moving, they asked to come along. Before leaving town, every stick of my belongings gets tossed into a dumpster. Upon departure, Garret and I took the lead, with Melvin and Ricky following Melvin's Corvette.

Before we leave Reno, Cal, and Mother had gotten back together, Grandfather had passed away from a heart attack, and Aunt Marylou had died of breast cancer.

Our first stop is in Las Vegas. Then it is on to the Grand Canyon for three weeks before heading to Flag Staff, Arizona, where we would stay another two weeks. From Flag Staff, it is a stopover in Albuquerque, New Mexico, for three more days and then onwards into Oklahoma. From there, we continued east; as we were passing through Little Rock, Arkansas, Melvin's Corvette started overheating. When we make a stop to inspect the trouble, I located the problem; the car engine had two cracked heads. Melvin felt it could make it into Memphis, Tennessee. In Memphis, again, I checked under the hood, and Melvin added more water to the radiator before continuing. Every stop reminded me of all the other times I had traveled the same highway.

The Corvette made it to Dixon, Tennessee, before blowing its head gaskets; we were thirty miles west of Nashville. Melvin coasted into a truck stop, and a tow truck is, hired to take the Corvette to a Dealership in Nashville.

Melvin and Ricky got into the car with Garret and me, and we continued following the tow truck into town. The Dealership had already closed by the time we reached it. However, the tow truck driver said he had a key to their shop, and he opened the enormous doors to pull into the garage. As soon as the car is, unhooked, the tow driver asked me.

"Are you Elvis?"

It is clear by the look on the driver's face that I am the real deal. Melvin and I walk back to the Corvette to get some personal items out of the car. While we do that, Ricky tells the tow driver,

"You know, the one you believe to be Elvis, well, he's Elvis Presley's cousin."

I ask the driver.

"Say, do you know of an excellent Hotel?"

The driver, "Sure man, you guys follow me; we'll go over to the Hall of Fame Motor Inn."

When we arrived at the Inn. The tow driver said he could get us a reasonable rate with me being the Cousin of Elvis and asked everyone to wait in the lobby while he goes up to the front desk. The driver tells the desk clerk.

"Don't make an issue, but the fellow standing over there is Elvis Presley's Cousin. Now, I do not want anybody to know he is here. Just give me their room keys."

With a hand motion, the driver got Melvin to come over to the check-in to sign the register. The Clerk handed him the keys and never asked him to show any I.D. While waiting, I could not help noticing the people sitting in the lobby. They were looking at me as if they were, seeing Elvis himself.

After settling into our rooms, Garret, Melvin, and I go down to the hotel bar. Ricky remains in the room. As we passed by the front desk, the Clerk nodded as we continued on our way to bellying up to the bar. The Bartender came over to take our drink orders when the bar phone rang; the Bartender excused himself and answered it. Returning, he said.

"Mr. Presley, welcome to the Hall of Fame."

Garret had already suggested that I play along to see how far the people would take it, and I said.

"Thank you; just do not tell the bar who I am."

Melvin started laughing when the Bartender answered.

"Nashville is full of celebrities who want to be low-keyed."

It is clear from the Bartender's conversation that the Clerk is on the other end of that ringing phone. How else would he have known to call me, Mr. Presley.

The Bartender brought the drinks, then went over and started talking to the cocktail server. When she makes her rounds, she tells all the other patrons that Elvis is sitting up at the bar, not his Cousin. Instantly I am surrounded chiefly by drunks telling me how much they like my movies and music.

Garret said to me.

"How dumb could these red necks be?"

By closing time, all three of us had enjoyed the evening drinking on the Presley's name, and the following day, Melvin said.

"What a bunch of jerks last night. Can you believe it; they thought you were Elvis. Shit, you could own this town just by hanging around idiots like we're in that bar."

I replied, "You might have something there, Melvin; it is easy to fool drunks. The bigger the lie, one tells the more who will believe it."

Our schedule for that day is to check on Melvin's car. At the Dealership, as expected, the car's engine head gaskets were, blown. When we leave there, Ricky, by purchasing a newspaper, looking for a place to live and find a house for rent on White Creek Pike.

We left town, headed north, and just over the Cumberland River Bridge, on Interstate 65, we exited Trinity Lane and continued west to White Creek Pike. About two miles up is the furnished three-bedroom rental; it fits our needs, and I rented it. After everyone settled in, I take Garret to the airport because he has a more pressing business in the East. Within a few days, Melvin and I had found work as electricians. When we left for work each day, Ricky stayed home. The more he spends at home, the more he becomes homesick for his father and mother; Finally, I put him on an airplane headed west.

One afternoon while Melvin and I are at the house, we had just returned home from the workday when a tornado came through. It is a warm day, with very little wind. Melvin is in the kitchen cooking a Chicken Pot Pie. I am outside, sitting on the front porch, looking at a newspaper. The wind picks up, and as I raise my head, I see over in a Wheatfield across the road, a funnel cloud heading straight towards me. I jumped up and ran inside the house. There I open all the windows and shut off all-electric in hopes the Tornado will pass through the house instead of destroying it.

Trying to explain that a Tornado is coming to Melvin was a moot issue, considering he thought I was pulling his leg. Melvin went into the living room carrying a Pot Pie; as he looked out the front window and saw the Tornado coming straight towards him, just as it is about to reach the house, bringing wind and water. I dove on the sofa just as debris started passing overhead. The Tornado exits out the rear of the house. Melvin comes out from behind a chair over in the corner, holding an empty container that once held his Pot Pie. The Tornado had taken the Pot Pie and left an immaculate box. However, it never touched Melvin. In its wake, there is, left extensive damage to the house and property, leaving Melvin and me no other choice than to find new lodging. We located a two-bedroom Cottage at the Monterey Hotel on Dickerson Road.

At the Monterey Hotel, I meet Gena Lee, and Melvin meets Sylvia. Also living on the property was Roy, a painter with his wife, Betty Lou, Gena Lee's sister. Besides Betty Lou, they had two other sisters and three brothers.

One evening over at Roy's Cottage, a few people gathered, and among them was Gena Lee. From that night, Gena Lee makes it a point to visit Roy and Betty as much as she finds the time. Before long, she and I are dating, and a month later, Melvin, Sylvia, Gena Lee, and I had rented a home on Riverside Drive in East Nashville.

Six months later, Garret and I had finished all contracts in Nashville; however, our following commitment is in Davis, California, where Garret had already gone to recon the contract. Near to Davis is Concord, and there is Northridge Apartments and is where Cal and Mother had gotten off to and were working as managers of the apartment complex. I called mother and mentioned I am coming to Davis. She made the offer that if Melvin and I would be interested in working in the complex, jobs are waiting. I brought Melvin and the girls the idea, and we all agreed we would go out to Northridge. I would have instead left Gena Lee in Nashville; however, she is pregnant.

Upon liquidating everything in Nashville, a few days later, we were driving into Northridge. Within a few days to rest up, I become the new apartment's maintenance man, and Melvin becomes the property's painter. Gena lee and Sylvia became the apartment's maids and renovators; when an apartment became vacant, the girls cleaned them for the following tenets.

Eight months after arriving at Northridge, Gena Lee gives birth to a boy child we named James. When Garret and I had finished our business in the Davis area, Garret heads back to Nashville. Melvin and Sylvia move to San Jose. Cal and Mother are, transferred to a complex in Reno, Nevada. I packed things up, and Gena Lee and our son headed back to Nashville, and I would meet up with Garret there.

We moved on Arrowood drive in the Cleve Hall area of south Nashville. It is a three-bedroom, two-bath home. Off the kitchen is a garage, converted into a recreational room, with a fireplace, bar, and entertainment stage.

With our Client clientele constant, money was coming in. However, I needed a proper job to cover my tracks, where I could take off from time to time and not get fired. Leave it to Garret; he got me a job as a building engineer for the Belle Mead Office Park on Harding Road in West Nashville.

Then, like a plague, Cal and Mother Show up at my door and stay until Garret found them employment as managers of an apartment complex in the Melrose district. Within a few months Melvin and Sylvia were next to show up, and they moved in with Cal and Mother. Shortly after them, from California come to the newlyweds Ricky and Terry. They, too, moved in with Cal and Mother.

Gena Lee, our life was getting along well and then she suggested we see a movie with its title having the same name as me. After that night, whatever lifestyle I had been given so far disappeared and it is as if I had stepped onto a roller coaster headed for hell.

End

Where the Roller Coaster ride takes me, and who I become, get: My Assumed Identity, Rocky's Story; by Jack Hayword.

Made in the USA
Middletown, DE
30 September 2021